For Reference

Not to be taken from this room

The Facts On File

Dictionary of New Words

Harold LeMay
Sid Lerner
Marian Taylor

First Published in paperback as
THE NEW NEW WORDS DICTIONARY
by Ballantine Books,
A Division of Random House, Inc.
Expanded for Facts On File

Facts On File
New York • Oxford

The Facts On File Dictionary of New Words

Facts On File, Inc.
460 Park Avenue South
New York, New York 10016

Published by arrangement with Ballantine Books, A Division of Random House, Inc.

British CIP data available on request
Facts On File books are available at special discounts when purchased in bulk quantities for businesses, associations, institutions, or sales promotion. Please contact the Special Sales Department at 212/683-2244. (Dial 1-800-322-8755, except in NY, AK, HI)

ISBN 0-8160-2088-4

Compositon by Facts On File/Maxwell Typographics

Printed in the United States of America

10 9 8 7 6 5 4 3 2 1

This book printed on acid-free paper.

Contents

Acknowledgments

The authors are grateful for advice and contributions from Marilyn Abraham; Juliann Barbato; Maria Behan; Donna Buffa; Larry Earle Bone; Harold I. Drucker; Nancy Garrett; Constance Jones; Helaine Lerner; Marla Maidenbaum; Abigail Meisel; Stanley Nass; Emily Rechnitz; Blake Taylor; Rachel Urquheart; J. Bud Feuchtwanger; and Nancy Toff.

Preface

New words are now entering the English language at an ever-increasing rate. Those of us who compile large dictionaries sift through tens of thousands of potential entries for each new edition. In the rapid ebb and flow of language, standard dictionaries cannot list all the words and expressions in frequent use at any one moment: to do so would require that a new dictionary be printed every week and that all the unimportant words and expressions that were coined to live for a day or a few weeks would need to be listed.

Even though the best standard dictionaries, such as the *Random House College Dictionary*, may be updated every two years, there is a necessary time lag in collecting and verifying new words and checking their exact pronunciations, meanings, uses, and etymologies, and then editing, proofreading, printing, and binding a large book. In addition, there are many ephèmeral words, short-lived catch phrases, slogans, and terms, in the news for a few days or weeks because they are attached to one political speech or news item, that are only of brief topical interest and are thus never entered in standard dictionaries. This leaves us with flurries of words and phrases scattered throughout our newspapers and magazines, rolling out of our radios and television sets, swirling through the air of our homes, workplaces, schools, and streets, which are not yet recorded or may never need be recorded in any authoritative dictionary.

Thus, there is a need for a small, informal book of new words, one that can be produced quickly and without consideration of the criteria and standards of authoritative dictionaries, a book for those who are interested in the latest words and expressions, whether or not these prove to be important or unimportant, long-lasting or just passing. This book attempts to fill that need. It is not meant to be a complete or even a precise coverage of new words and expressions but is for those who need or want to have a good sampling of them even before they can be pinned down as to importance or exact use. The authors of this book do not pretend to be professional lexicographers and do not attempt to be arbiters in the world of today's neologisms. They do not promise that their work is based on the vast citation files, a staff of experienced dictionary editors and consultants, or the years of research, checking, and painstaking editing needed to create major dictionaries. They do, however, promise to be alert, to serve as part of an early-warning system of new terms that may become important in the language, and to attempt informal definitions from the first imprecise evidence while the terms may still be emerging and not fully formed.

The Facts On File Dictionary of New Words promises only one thing: to be interesting to all those who want to keep abreast—right now—of our constantly changing language. It will be useful to all who want to know at least the preliminary meaning of current new terms, whether or not all these terms will be needed tomorrow as well as today, and useful to those who want advance warning of words that may enter our standard dictionaries after they have proved their usefulness and been pinned down more exactly.

This, then, is an informal, unscientific sampling of important, or often merely interesting, new words and expressions. It will make every reader more aware of our ever-changing vocabulary, of the fluctuation of words in modern life. It will also make every reader more aware of, and better able to talk and write about, current events, trends, and fads, better able to keep up with today's world by becoming aware of today's words.

Stuart Flexner

Introduction

This book is an eclectic assemblage of new words currently used by people of all ages, in all professions, and at all economic levels. As we go to press, few of these words—with their up-to-the-minute meanings—appear in any of the superb college dictionaries now available, not even in the 1987 unabridged edition of the *Random House Dictionary of the English Language*. We make no claim to listing *all* the not-yet-dictionaried words in use; we do claim that sooner or later you will run into many of these words in everyday contexts.

In the first edition of the *Dictionary of New Words*, published in 1985, we predicted that "some of the words in this book will take root in the language and will appear in the upcoming major dictionaries." It seems we got that right: almost half of the new words in the first *DNW* found their way into the mighty new *Random House* and, therefore, were edited out of this edition. Even if a word has a short life, however, it's important to know what it means while it is appearing in headlines and talk shows. The words and phrases in this book are in frequent use *now*. Not to understand them puts us at risk of not fully understanding the world we live in.

In gathering words for this book, we have reviewed newspapers, magazines, books, pamphlets, labels, and catalogues. We have listened to radio and television, to conversations on trains, at sports arenas, rock concerts, and computer conventions. We have consulted experts in many fields. Our hardest job was not finding and defining new words; it was finding, defining and not *including* certain new words. The slang words and phrases we have chosen, for example, we encountered in places like *The Wall Street Journal* and TV's *60 Minutes*, as well as on the street. There are, of course, hundreds of others, many of which, if they survive long enough to be recorded, will find homes in future compilations of colloquialisms. Some of these, which we heard often but not quite often enough were: *living large* (on top of the world; life at its best), *noid* (worry unnecessarily; probably derived from *paranoid*, as in "Don't noid at the way he looked at you"), and *in traffic* (in the fast lane).

Other words absent from these pages are most of those in the "inside" lexicons of special or technical fields. Take medicine: We accepted *gomer* and *box* but left out a book's worth of expressions used by doctors in sentences like this one from a *New York Times* column by Perri Klass: "Mrs. Tolstoy is your basic LOL in NAD, admitted for a soft ruleout MI." (Translation: Mrs. T. is a Little Old Lady in No Apparent Distress who is in the hospital to make sure she has not had a heart attack [rule out Myocardial Infarction].)

Or, in the computer world, for instance, we assumed that people who need to know the new words spawned daily either already know them or will use one of the many techno-specific books about them, and therefore we have not included many. Exceptions are such terms as *phreaking, cracker, base-band,* and *electronic cottage,* which have migrated from the narrow streams of their conception to the mainstream of popular language.

We have also left out many new words spun off *other* new words. From the *Couch Potato* phenomenon, for example, have sprung such coinages as *spudismo, vidspud,* and *transcendental vegetation*—all choice but not likely to survive the tuber-emblazoned T-shirts, banners, hats, buttons, and other potatophernalia accompanying the potatomania of the late eighties. Another float of transient words and expressions springs from government and military sources. Particularly hard to reject were newspeak phrases like "terminate with extreme prejudice" for *kill,* "permanent prehostility" for *peacetime,* "predawn vertical insertion" for *early-morning airborne invasion,* and "controlled flight into terrain" for *plane crash.*

New words and expressions sometimes materialize out of thin air, dominate headlines and news broadcasts for an hour or a month, then disappear into the limbo of yesterday's *lingo.* Such a phrase was 1987's *Dodge City loophole.* Applied to Florida's astonishingly permissive new gun law—which allowed anyone to carry firearms openly—the *loophole* looked like a serious contender for these pages. When Florida's legislature prudently closed the loophole only nine days after opening it, however, we prudently shot it down as an entry.

The words that do, at last, appear in this book are likely to pop up anywhere. Readers will already know what some of them mean. We guarantee that none of you will know them all. We have not *decided* what these words mean; we are merely reporting that they are currently used in certain ways to mean certain specific things. Some readers may dispute our definitions or have additional meanings for these words. We'd like to hear from you. In the next edition, we'll use appropriate additions and suggestions you send us.

A

acid wash *(noun)*
The process of washing jeans in chlorine to soften the fabric and produce a streaked, worn look. After the stiffening resin is stripped from the material, the clothing is washed in a machine with fist-size pumice stones impregnated with chlorine solution, which removes some of the dye and leaves the garment lighter in color with white spots and streaks—inspiring the name "acid wash," although no acid is actually used.

Activase TPA *(noun)*
Introduced by Genentech in 1988, Activase TPA is a biotech drug that dissolves blood clots that damage heart muscles.

ACT UP *(noun)*
Acronym for Aids Coalition to Unleash Power. Founded by playwright Larry Kramer to press for increased government involvement in the fight against the AIDS epidemic; ACT UP deliberately focuses on the homosexual aspect of the disease, employing confrontational demonstrations known as *zaps*.

ADRMP *(noun)*
Acronym for automatic dialing recorded message program. A computer-software program used in telemarketing, ADRMPs can dial hundreds of telephone numbers per day to make a recorded sales pitch. As a result of public complaints, many states are passing legislation against the practice.

advid ADD-vid *(noun)*
An advertising videotape, most frequently used to demonstrate the strong points of an applicant for college or a job. In 1988 U.S. colleges and universities reported receiving advids from about 5 percent of their would-be freshmen or graduate students.

aeroshell *(noun)*
The outer structure for the aerospace vehicle scheduled to replace the space shuttle by the year 2000. Covered by the aeroshell, the new vehicle will be lightweight, rocket-propelled, reusable, and functional under all weather conditions, announced the National Aeronautics and Space Administration (NASA).

affinity card *(noun)*
A bank credit card offered in conjunction with a nonprofit or charitable organization. Banks that sponsor affinity cards donate a percentage of all purchases charged with the cards to such organizations as the March of Dimes, the Sierra Club, or one of the political parties.

afterburst *(noun)*
The phenomenon presumed to follow a nuclear war, in which radioactivity would be released into the earth's atmosphere, water, and soil, as well as into the tissues of all animal and plant life, there to remain indefinitely.

Afro-pop *(noun)*
Contemporary African music that incorporates traditional elements and instruments in combination with such electronic devices as synthesizers and electric guitars.

Agenda™ *(noun)*
One of a new generation of computer software dubbed by its maker "a personal information manager." Using aspects of traditional programs without their rigid rules, these new systems enable users to compile and correlate huge amounts of information into personal data bases.

aging gene   *(noun)*
Term used by medical researchers for the as-yet-unidentified substance that creates the signs of old age in mammals: gray hair, wrinkles, brittle bones, menopause, etc.

agita   AJ-it-uh   *(noun)*
An Italian word meaning, simply, acid indigestion. Agita is gaining currency as a description of the distress induced by unpleasant social circumstances, such as dealing with an overbearing boss or anticipating the visit of one's mother-in-law.

agrigenetics   *(noun)*
Biotechnical research in plant breeding; the attempt to control plant evolution by genetic manipulation and gene splicing to provide desirable new varieties, such as a (still experimental) strain of wheat with the soybean's capability of fertilizing its own roots with airborne nitrogen. Agrigeneticists have produced such new agricultural items as a redder, less watery commercial tomato and disease-resistant sugar cane.

agrimation   *(noun)*
A compound of *agri*culture and auto*mation*. The use of sophisticated robots in farming to do work requiring judgment and sensitive dexterity formerly possible only with human labor—from harvesting crops to caring for a dairy herd.

aircraft carrier   *(noun)*
A star basketball center who excels at handling the ball, making baskets, and playing defense.

akachochin   *(noun)*
Japanese for red-lantern restaurant, from the traditional red paper lantern that hangs in front. An akachochin is a small establishment, often only a counter with stools, sometimes outdoors, that serves sake, beer, and yakitori (charcoal-broiled chicken).

A-list   *(noun)*
The most important people in a specific field; thus, in Washington, D.C., the A-list might include the top-ranking

members of the diplomatic corps, the nation's most powerful politicians, and the city's leading socialites. A Manhattan A-list would not only consist of high-society figures but real-estate barons and Broadway luminaries. The Barbra Streisand film *Nuts*, said *Newsweek*, was "a classic example of A-list Hollywood turning out what it thinks is Important Entertainment."

all hat and no cattle   *(colloquialism)*
A descriptive phrase from the American Southwest, applying to a person whose assets are mostly on the surface.

alley apple   *(noun)*
A slang term meaning a loose brick or rock, especially when the brick is used as a projectile.

allophone   *(noun)*
any person who does not speak French, especially in Canada, where the use of French, particularly in government communications, is an important political issue.

ambisonic   am-buh-SON-ik   *(adjective)*
Describing a form of high-fidelity sound reproduction that, by electronically simulating the directional attributes of the sound waves it disseminates, gives the listener the impression he is in the center of a group of instruments or singers. Ambisonic music is sometimes called "surround sound."

American Eagle   *(noun)*
The gold and silver bullion coin issued by the U.S. Mint. The one- ounce and one-half-ounce gold coins are 91.6 percent gold and are engraved with the figure of Liberty by sculptor Augustus Saint- Gaudens with the American eagle on the reverse. The face of the one- ounce silver coin features A.A. Weinman's "Walking Liberty," which appeared on the silver half-dollar from 1916 to 1947.

animal   *(noun)*
Politicians' and journalists' term for a reporter, technician, or photographer who accompanies candidates on flying campaign trips. Animals are a shade lower in the hierarchy of the

trade than the politicians and top-level newspeople whom they often follow in a "zoo plane," a second, far less luxurious aircraft than that allotted their colleagues.

animal rights movement   *(noun)*
A burgeoning worldwide crusade that teaches that the pleasure or pain felt by animals is as important as the pleasure or pain felt by human beings. Animal rights activists have launched recent strenuous campaigns against laboratory experimentation on animals, seal hunting, and *factory farming.*

ankle   *(verb)*
Slang expression meaning to quit, to leave a job. "Peter Trueman, news anchor at indie Global TV web for 15 years, has ankled effective June 30." (*Variety*)

anti-sense medicine   *(noun)*
An experimental science that looks to target and block bad genes, such as cancer-causing oncogenes, much as correcting tape blocks out a typographical error. By using an inverted piece of the gene code to lock onto potentially dangerous genetic messengers, their ability to cause harm can be canceled out.

appliance garage   *(noun)*
A custom kitchen cabinet designed expressly to house small, frequently used appliances.

Arabsat   *(noun)*
A radio-relay satellite owned by the Arab Satellite Communications Organization.

arb   *(noun)*
Abbreviation for arbitrageur, or risk arbitrageur, a Wall Street trader who seeks profits from buying and quickly selling stocks in companies that announce merger plans.

arena football   *(noun)*
A version of football played indoors on an artificial turf field measuring 150 x 85 feet (half the size of a regulation field). The

field boasts high nets on either side of nine-foot-wide goalposts and foam-padded sideline barriers like hockey boards. Eight players on each side play both offense and defense with the exception of the quarterback and kicker; missed field goals bounce off the end-zone nets and back into play, and the clock runs as in hockey, stopping only for time outs, substitutions, scores, penalties, and injuries.

Argentine method   *(noun)*
The practice in some Latin American countries of secretly kidnapping and executing people without trial. So-called from the "dirty war" in which government death squads "disappeared" more than 12,000 Argentines suspected of undesirable political activity.

aristology   *(noun)*
"The science of dining or the art of eating well," according to food authority Craig Claiborne, who quotes an essay on aristology asserting that "the number of guests at a meal should not exceed eight and ideally there should be only six so that the conversation may be general."

Arkie   *(noun)*
The computer-games industry's equivalent of an Oscar. Arkie winners are selected by a reader poll conducted by *Electronic Games* magazine.

arms supermarket   *(noun)*
An international arrangement designed to supply arms to the Nicaraguan contras. *Newsweek* defined the market as "an unlikely partnership involving longtime CIA arms merchants, agents of the Israeli Mossad secret service and the intelligence arm of the Honduran military . . . financed at least in part with drug money."

aromatherapy   *(noun)*
Introduced as an exclusive treatment with aromatic facials of floral and herbal masks individually blended to harmonize with a particular client's skin type, aromatherpy was said by *Vogue* to be "aimed at energizing or calming the skin *and* the

spirits." Now major cosmetics firms have come out with mass-market fragrances that are, they claim, scientifically proven to affect people's moods and behavior.

Artagraph *(noun)*

A patented process for reproducing oil paintings with extremely high fidelity. A laser light-filtering technique is used to copy the colors, which are printed on an oil-based foil and heat-transferred onto canvas. The facsimile has exactly the same texture as the original, with brush strokes, impasto, or palette-knife applications all faithfully duplicated, and finer color reproduction than has ever before been possible. The Artagraph process has been used by A.R.T., Inc., of Toronto to copy masterpieces at Britain's National Gallery and the Hermitage museum in Russia.

artificial gill *(noun)*

An experimental system for extracting oxygen from seawater; its future application is expected to be in making available unlimited oxygen supplies for divers and submarines.

artspeak *(noun)*

The vocabulary used by those hoping to sound knowledgeable about art. Artspeak, says artist, lecturer, and wit William Quinn, allows you to "sound halfway intelligent about art when you're not." Quinn, who teaches New Yorkers how to talk at art galleries and museums, advises his students to avoid such terms as "incredible," "cool," and "totally awesome." "Interesting" is a more effective word, he says, "especially when uttered with the head cocked and a hand cupping the chin contemplatively."

artsport *(noun)*

A form of modern dance that uses movements usually associated with athletics or gymnastics.

asham uh-SHAHM *(noun)*

A Jamaican powdered confection made from grinding together brown sugar and dried roasted corn.

A68 *(noun)*
A protein present in the brains of Alzheimer's disease patients. After identifying the protein in late 1987, medical researchers reported that its presence will prove useful in the early diagnosis of Alzheimer's, the devastating brain disorder that causes dementia and memory loss in millions of people.

astroponics *(noun)*
Space agriculture. Astroponic researchers hope to develop techniques that will ensure production of healthy plants aboard spacecraft, space stations, and on lunar bases. Such vegetation, the scientists say, will recycle wastes and replenish oxygen and water as well as supply food at space outposts. Prospective astroponic crops include lettuce, wheat, soybeans, potatoes, and sugar beets.

atemoya ah-tuh-MOY-uh *(noun)*
A hybrid variety of the tropical sugar apple, which is too fragile to be shipped commercially. The atemoya is not as sweet as the sugar apple, or sweetsop, but its firmer flesh allows it to be transported to the distant markets where it is becoming popular.

Atrovent™ *(noun)*
Trademarked name of a new drug said to give major relief from the common cold. Atrovent, a nasal spray, inhibits the action of a chemical that causes runny noses, but does not produce drowsiness.

Automation Alley *(noun)*
Nickname for the area between Ann Arbor and Detroit, Michigan, America's leading robotics production center.

Auto Shade™ *(noun)*
The trademarked name of a folding cardboard sun shade for automobiles. The shade is designed to fit inside the windshield on top of the dash in a parked car to keep the steering wheel and the front seat cool. The Auto Shade was developed in Israel and is popular in the Mediterranean area as an advertising

giveaway, but in the U.S. it is selling for its function and often comes decorated with a giant pair of sunglasses.

AX-5   *(noun)*
An experimental all-aluminum spacesuit. (See tin man and Mark-3.)

B

backpack nuke *(noun)*
A lightweight nuclear bomb properly known as a Special Atomic Demolition Munitions System. Each backpack bomb weighs about sixty pounds and can be carried by one person. It is capable of destroying a target as large as a major airfield but is primarily designed to take out dams, bridges, and power plants.

Bambi syndrome *(noun)*
The condition resulting when wild animals, usually those in national parks, are treated by tourists as though they were Disney-style pets, with the result that the animals become dangerously "friendly." Some authorities attribute an increase in bear attacks to this syndrome.

bammie *(noun)*
A Jamaican cassava bread baked from grated cassava, usually in a flat, round loaf.

B and T crowd *(noun)*
A disparaging New York City term for people who must use bridges and tunnels to get in and out of Manhattan.

banger *(noun)*
A drink consisting of vodka and ice in a glass, which the consumer is supposed to bang once on the bar before quaffing in one gulp.

barter advertising *(noun)*
The television-industry practice of trading programming for commercial air time. In barter advertising, the producers provide a show or a first-run series to individual stations in exchange for commercial time, which is then sold to advertisers.

b-boy, b-girl *(noun)*
A devotee of rap music, possibly derived from "break" for "break-dance."

baseband *(noun)*
A local area network of personal computers interconnected by wire similar to a telephone system. Designed to link a company's equipment together for efficient utilization and to cut costs by eliminating duplication of machines and peripherals, the network allows the computers to transmit data to one another.

battered wife syndrome *(noun)*
The extensive physical injuries exhibited by women repeatedly abused by their husbands or lovers.

bazuko bah-ZOO-koh *(noun)*
A cocaine-based drug similar to crack but even more potent and extremely addictive. A concoction of coca-leaf paste, kerosene, and ether, the powder is smoked in cigarettes. Its explosive impact earned the name—from bazooka. It is cheaper than crack and very dangerous.

beat sweetener *(noun)*
A flattering news story written by Washington-beat reporters, to reward sources for leaking inside information.

beer ball *(noun)*
A plastic sphere holding 5.16 gallons of beer. Beer balls, which are promoted for the family-picnic and outdoor-activities markets, come packaged in watertight boxes designed to hold ice.

Belgian Blue *(noun)*
A very muscular European breed of cattle that is at the heart of an attempt to create a leaner type of beef using biotechnology. Inseminating American stock with imported Belgian Blue semen produces a crossbreed that yields beef lower in fat, cholesterol, and calories than chicken.

bellini   buh-LEEN-ee *(noun)*
A popular summer drink consisting of two parts champagne to one part peach nectar.

belt bag *(noun)*
The so-called "fanny packs" popular with skiers and hikers have crossed over into city use as a substitute for handbags for casual wear. Strapped around the waist, they leave the hands free and make things difficult for purse snatchers and pickpockets.

beltway bandit *(noun)*
A Washington, D.C., epithet, applied to former Pentagon officials and retired senior officers who work as weapons and procurement consultants, and who often operate from offices in the suburban beltway vicinity.

BEV *(noun)*
Acronym for black English vernacular. Also known to educators as Ebonics—a contraction of "ebony" and "phonics"—BEV is an informal version of standard English widely used in the American black community.

Big Floyd *(noun)*
An FBI computer network capable of evaluating crime reports and of formulating lines of investigation based on its data. Some civil libertarians fear that if other government-agency files are

shared with the FBI, the potential exists for the creation of a "Big Brother."

big whip *(interjection)*
Similar to "big deal" to indicate disdain for the importance of something. "So you've got a new car—big whip!"

biobelt *(noun)*
A telemetry device worn by an astronaut around the waist to record and transmit data to mission control on his or her physiological processes.

biobone *(noun)*
A filter material made from pulverized chicken bone for reclaiming rennin from milk in cheese processing. Rennin is an enzyme used to curdle milk, essential in cheese manufacturing, and is ordinarily lost in solution. The porous biobone salvages the rennin for reuse.

biochip *(noun)*
A computer composed of living bacteria. Genetic scientists, who hope to produce a working biochip by the early 1990s, say the new devices will make the microprocessors of the future ten million times as efficient as the computers now in use. A major asset of the biochip, its developers assert, will be its ability to repair its own malfunctions.

bioremediation *(noun)*
The technique of using genetically engineered microbes to destroy toxic chemicals in hazardous waste.

birdcage *(noun)*
The traffic-controlled air space over an airport—so dubbed from its shape and the planes, or "birds," contained in it.

blackened fish *(noun)*
A popular item in Cajun cuisine, consisting of pieces of fish charred on a very hot griddle or in a very hot skillet after being coated with a mixture that includes red and white pepper and garlic.

Black Monday *(noun)*
October 19, 1987, when the Dow Jones Industrial Average tumbled a record of 22.6 percent, precipitating a worldwide stock-market crash.

black spot *(noun)*
A black-populated village in South Africa that is isolated within a larger white community. One of the stated goals of the nation's apartheid policy is to eliminate such areas by moving their residents into the "homelands" that are reserved for blacks and that constitute 14 percent of South Africa's territory.

black tar *(noun)*
A new type of heroin from northern Mexico processed from locally grown opium poppies. A simplified process gives it its characteristic tarry look and consistency and results in high purity and low price. Because it is difficult to dilute, users get it in a very potent form, causing increased overdose deaths.

blaff *(noun)*
A fish stew from the West Indies, usually made with vegetables and seasoned with garlic.

blazing seat *(noun)*
An electrical device made in Israel that delivers a shock similar to that of the police stun gun. Blazing seats are being installed under passenger seats in Parisian taxis to protect drivers against robbers and muggers.

bloodless surgery *(noun)*
Basically, an operation performed without any transfusion. This experimental form of surgery has become more interesting as people have become increasingly concerned about blood-borne diseases ranging from hepatitis to AIDS.

blood scavenger *(noun)*
A machine used in surgery that suctions off some blood, then filters, washes, and returns it to the patient.

blue-corn chips   *(noun)*
Trendy snack chips made from cornmeal processed from blue corn. Originally available in health food and gourmet stores, they are gaining an increasing share of the general snack-food market.

blush wine   *(noun)*
Pink wines made from red grapes. Blushes are prevented from turning red by the removal of the skins from the grape juice, producing a light pink wine that tastes like a white wine.

blow off   *(verb)*
Slang term for cancel, or fail to appear. "Did you go to court for that traffic ticket?" "No, I blew it off. I'll just pay the fine."

boarder baby   *(noun)*
A healthy but abandoned infant whose early life is spent in a hospital.

bodybuilder's psychosis   *(noun)*
A mental disorder suffered by some athletes who use excessive quantities of steroids to gain weight and build muscles. Its symptoms, which usually stop with the cessation of drug intake, range from delusions of grandeur to paranoia, depression, and hallucinatory voices.

bodywash   *(verb)*
To "launder" the combat death of military personnel killed in covert action in officially "peaceful" countries or diplomatically sensitive areas by arranging a fake fatal accident somewhere else.

bogart   *(verb)*
In black English vernacular, to bogart is to act in a blustering, intimidating way, as tough guy Humphrey Bogart did.

Boinks   *(noun)*
Small flexible plastic tubes marketed as toys by Endless Possibilities Inc. The brightly colored Boinks may be compressed,

springlike, to fly harmlessly across rooms, or bent into bracelets or anklets.

bomb blanket *(noun)*
An explosive-suppression device used by bomb-disposal squads. Bomb blankets are woven from Kevlar, the material used in bulletproof vests. If an explosion takes place under the blanket, the blanket rises into a dome, containing the force of the blast.

boomer *(noun)*
Informal name for a ballistic-missile nuclear submarine.

boomerang *(noun)*
Slang for a grown child who has lived away from home and returns to live with his or her parents. *New York* magazine reported in early 1988: "Social scientists have started to identify this return to the nest as an important national trend."

boruga *(noun)*
A yogurt drink originating in the Dominican Republic and now being distributed in the U.S., it is a creamy, sweet drink with "natural flavoring."

botanica   bott-ANN-uh-kuh *(noun)*
A small Hispanic drug store dealing in herbs and devotional objects for religious and superstitious practices, especially those rooted in Afro-Caribbean culture.

boudoir photography *(noun)*
A fast-growing new service by photographic studios that provides individuals with intimate to near-nude pictures of themselves to present to lovers or spouses, often to revive a romance.

Bowash *(noun)*
Real estate and business term for the Boston-to-Washington corridor.

box   *(verb)*
Medical for *die*. "Any action in 612?" "Yeah. He boxed around midnight."

bracketing   *(noun)*
A technique used in election campaigns to neutralize the opposition. In bracketing, aides are sent into a city where a rival candidate is to appear; there, before the rival's speech, the aides question his or her record. After the speech, the aides remain to refute the candidate's positions.

branded diamond   *(noun)*
A gemstone inscribed with a number and trademark. Diamond branding is a new process made possible by recently developed laser technology. Claiming a "real surge of interest in documented diamonds," in late 1987 one industry spokesman credited it to "the consumer movement toward buying high quality."

breakup value   *(noun)*
The worth of a company after it is dismembered and its divisions sold separately. "The concept of breakup value," said *The Wall Street Journal* in 1987, "came into prominence as a direct by-product of the feverish take-over boom" of the 1980s.

brew pub   *(noun)*
A restaurant or bar that brews its own beer on the premises.

B-strep   *(noun)*
Abbreviation for Group B streptococcus, a bacteria responsible for a growing percentage of deaths among newborn infants. The organism lives in the gastrointestinal tract and is sometimes passed on to the baby via the birth canal. Both men and women may be carriers of B- strep; current medical research indicates that the organism is probably sexually transmitted. If not treated in time, the infection is fatal for at least half its victims.

Bubba Law   *(noun)*
Recently passed legislation in Texas that mandates that a policeman cannot stop and ticket a motorist for having an open

container of beer or hard liquor unless he clearly sees the driver drinking an obviously alcoholic beverage. The law gets its popular name from the "good ol' boys" who fought tough drinking-and-driving legislation. Camouflage plastic beer-can covers, which make the cans look like soft drinks, have become popular in some areas.

bubble   *(noun)*
A "safe room" within a room, designed to be bugproof, i.e., secure against electronic listening devices.

bubble concept   *(noun)*
An Environmental Protection Agency measurement that considers the total industrial pollution created by a factory rather than each individual contaminant. The concept envisions a bubble above the building that has a single aperture that vents all the effluvia released by the factory.

buildering   *(noun)*
The sport of climbing the outside of tall buildings, using rock-climbing techniques. Buildering is a variation on bouldering, an elementary form of climbing whose enthusiasts learn technique at a relatively safe height.

bump-and-run   *(noun)*
An option in football wherein a pass receiver may block a defensive player before going downfield to receive a pass.

bum-rush   *(verb)*
To invade, break down the doors to get in; a reversal of "bum's rush" for *eject*.

buppie   *(noun)*
Acronym for black urban professional.

bus   *(noun)*
The top-secret component of a new computer design under development by a consortium of personal-computer manufacturers. Bus hardware shuttles data between different parts of

the PC like a high-speed electronic transit system; its creators expect it to revolutionize the PC industry.

butterfly effect   *(noun)*
The production of a major occurrence by a minor one. Explaining the theory in a 1987 *Newsweek* article, meteorologist Edward Lorenz, discoverer of the butterfly effect, said: "If a butterfly flapped its wings in Brazil, it might produce a tornado in Texas. Unlikely as it seems, the tiny air currents that a butterfly creates travel across thousands of miles, jostling other breezes as they go and eventually changing the weather."

C

cafeteria plan *(noun)*
A flexible benefit package offered by some corporations to their employees that makes alternative options available in addition to such basic benefits as health insurance. Within a specified dollar amount, workers are able to tailor their own benefits programs to include features ranging from cash to legal services to extra vacation time.

Cajun popcorn *(noun)*
Fried cornmeal batter containing flakes of shrimp, crab, or crayfish. Cajun popcorn is a mainstay of Cajun cooking, a popular, highly spiced type of food that evolved in the Louisiana bayou country among the descendants of the Acadians—French-Canadians who were driven out of Nova Scotia by the British in the eighteenth century.

camel *(verb)*
To act in an uninspired and bureaucratic manner. Based on the humorous definition of a camel: a horse designed by a committee. Columnist William Safire quotes a disparaging remark about unimaginative people who, "afraid of change," are likely to "camel an idea to death."

camo *(noun)*
Green-and-brown-mottled fabric patterns similar to those used in military camouflage.

CAMP   *(noun)*
Acronym for Campaign Against Marijuana Planting, an American state-local-federal task force whose field teams search out and destroy illegàlly raised cannabis crops.

capoeira   cap-oh-EER-uh   *(noun)*
A ritual fighting dance originating in southwestern Africa and introduced into Brazil by African slaves in the 19th century. Resembling a cross between martial arts and breakdancing, capoeira has endured as a part of Brazilian cultural heritage and is currently fostered in the United States by the Capoeira Foundation of New York City.

capsule hotel   *(noun)*
Low-cost hotels in Japan in which the accommodations—cubicles about the size of a pup tent—are stacked like mail boxes in a post office. Each four-foot-high capsule, which contains a single bed, a clock-radio, a TV set and a reading light, costs about $24.00 a night.

caramel   *(noun)*
Fuel used in some nuclear reactors, composed of low-grade, enriched uranium and so called because of its resemblance to caramel candy.

cardiomyoplasty   *(noun)*
An experimental surgical procedure that replaces damaged heart tissue, most often as a result of a heart attack, with muscle tissue from another part of the patient's body.

Caridex™   *(noun)*
A chemical tooth-decay treatment system that dissolves the decayed part of a tooth and allows it to be washed away painlessly, without the need for drilling or anesthesia.

cascade   *(verb)*
In business-management jargon, to disseminate information rapidly throughout an organization.

CASE *(noun)*
Acronym for computer-aided software engineering. CASE is the technology that produces programs for the design of software and for translating these designs into computer code.

cassingle *(noun)*
A cassette single containing only a half hour of music with several variations of the same song.

cavaillon KAV-uh-yon *(noun)*
An intensely fragrant melon resembling a canteloupe. Imported from France, the cavaillon has become popular with elegant restaurants and their patrons despite its high price.

CD4 *(noun)*
An experimental anti-AIDS protein currently under development by medical researchers in the United States and Switzerland. CD4 is expected to combat the AIDS virus HIV by flooding the body of a victim with false targets, thereby diverting the virus from its natural course of attack. Scientists announced in early 1988 that U.S. clinical trials of the newly identified protein were being planned; before CD4 could be administered to human beings, however, the researchers said that months of animal testing and subsequent regulatory approval would be required.

CD-I *(noun)*
Interactive computer disk. Still in the developmental stage, these disks will allow the user to "talk back" to a television set to get information. Already in use commercially, home versions may be available in 1989.

CD-ROM *(noun)*
Computer Disk-Read Only Memory. A new combining of compact disk and computer technology that drastically increases the storage capacity of a computer. "A CD-ROM is a 5 1/4 inch laser disk that contains the same amount of information as 1,200 floppy disks." (*The New York Times*)

CD-videos   *(noun)*
Compact disks that are combined with video so that people can watch as well as listen to music. Leading U.S. electronic companies produce the hardware to play CD-videos, which can also be played on standard disk players, with sound only.

CENTS   *(noun)*
Acronym for the Consortium for the Education of Non-Trad tional Students. Formed by a group of New England colleg CENTS aims at attracting older, financially solvent students help boost falling enrollment and resulting losses in tuit income and state aid.

C-4   *(noun)*
An odorless, colorless plastic substance used in explos Reporting on the destruction of a Korean Air Boeing 707 i 1987, *Newsweek* said: "U.S. terrorism experts suspecte bomb on flight 858 [which killed its crew and 115 passe may have come from a new generation of explosives th miniaturized electronics and ... plastics such as C-4, wh virtually undetectable by conventional methods." The explosives, added the magazine, "can be stuffed into p worn as shoelaces, even hidden in the hair."

chaos   *(noun)*
A new branch of science based on the concept that se random events are governed by precise laws. Jame author of the 1987–88 best-selling book *Chaos: Maki Science,* asserts that chaos offers "a new way of findin systems that seem to have no order at all." Reviewin book, *The New York Times* called chaos "a science of things—of art and economics, of biological rhythms jams, of waterfalls and weather."

chatcom   *(noun)*
A radio or TV talk show whose main thrust is com Carson's *Tonight* show is an example.

checkbook journalism   *(noun)*
The reporting of news obtained through the payment of a fee for information; the phrase is usually one of contempt, implying the use of a less than straightforward means of gathering news.

checkbook witness   *(noun)*
An expert who is paid by the defense or prosecution to provide information at a court trial.

checkerboarding   *(verb)*
Local television station practice of running a different half-hour situation comedy nightly during the prime access time 7:30 to 8:00 P.M.

cheers   *(noun)*
A rapping, clapping, foot-stamping game that has become popular on the sidewalks of many Brooklyn neighborhoods. "It draws from cheers the youngsters have learned in school, rap music, traditional childhood games and their own experiences." (*The New York Times*)

chemfet   *(noun)*
Acronym for chemical field effect transistor, an experimental biosensor small enough to be placed inside the body to gather and analyze data, which it communicates to a remote computer.

chicken hawk   *(noun)*
A dedicated anticommunist who nevertheless managed to avoid active military service in the Vietnam War through such stratagems as alleged physical ailment, college deferment or the influence of powerful friends.

chicken run   *(noun)*
Derogatory term for the mass departure of refugees from places in the throes of civil unrest, especially South Africa.

chopsocky   *(noun)*
Showbiz term for a low-budget action film featuring martial-arts violence.

Christian pop   *(noun)*

Also known as "heavenly metal" and "evangelical pop," Christian pop is a form of rock music that preaches salvation. Annual record sales of the genre, which sprang from the "Jesus movement" of the late 1960s, had topped $300 million by the end of 1987. "Many evangelists say that rock music is of the devil," observed one Christian pop producer, "but thousands of kids come to our concerts and get their lives straightened out."

chronopharmacology   *(noun)*

The study of the relationship between drug dosage and body rhythms in the daily time cycle. Changes in bodily functions throughout the day can have a profound effect on the efficacy of medication, especially in the treatment of cancer with chemotherapy.

churn and burn   *(adjective)*

Term used to characterize a type of investment fraud in which, once a mark—the unsuspecting customer—has been enticed into an investment, the broker encourages him to keep changing to more promising hot prospects. The con artist takes a 10 percent commission on each transaction until all the money is gone.

cigarette   *(noun)*

A big, deep-vee high-speed powerboat patterned after the successful ocean-racing speedboat of that name developed by designer Don Aranow.

clamshell   *(noun)*

The hinged foam-plastic or cardboard boxes used to package sandwiches by such fast-food restaurants as McDonald's or Burger King. In early 1988 the plastic versions came under fire from New York's Mayor Koch because they are not biodegradable, contributing to greater waste pollution.

Claymation™   *(noun)*

The process (clay animation) of making animated movies with clay figures. The technique creates the illusion of motion by making many small adjustments to modeled clay figures between each frame of film.

climbing wall   *(noun)*
A man-made vertical wall with adjustable footholds and handholds used by sports climbers in international competitions.

clonidine   *(noun)*
An experimental drug reported to have marked success in curbing smokers' tobacco cravings. "Researchers," reports *Business Week*, "say the drug stops the urge [to smoke] directly by acting on those cells in the brain that are associated with addiction." Clonidine was first used in the treatment of hypertension.

clotbuster   *(noun)*
One of a new class of drugs that dissolves blood clots, a principal cause of heart attacks. Because of such clotbusters as streptokinase and TPA (tissue plasminogen activator), said prominent cardiologist George Beller in 1988, "thousands of lives will be saved next year that wouldn't have been in previous years."

cocooning   *(noun)*
The spending of leisure time in the comfort of the home rather than in restaurants, theaters, or other public places of amusement. In extreme cases, cocooning approaches a retreat from the harsh world into the safety of the hearth.

coke bugs   *(noun)*
Nickname for a cocaine-user's hallucination which convinces its victims that insects are crawling on them or coming out of their skin.

competitor analyst   *(noun)*
Euphemism for an industrial or corporate spy, a professional sleuth hired to discover a rival company's production methods and plans.

computer hedgehog   *(noun)*
An individual whose computer knowledge is limited to only one type of machine, activity, or set of programs.

computer monitoring   *(noun)*
A management technique for checking employee performance by connecting factory or office work stations to computers that count and record such activities as keystrokes per hour or time spent using telephone lines. *U.S. News and World Report* predicts that by 1990 more than half of the forty million U.S. workers expected to be using video display terminals will be subject to monitoring. While many employers are enthusiastic about the advantages of the practice, many employees are not. One union steward, for example, reflecting a widely held worker opinion, said, "It's like Big Brother watching you."

confrotalk   *(noun)*
Confrontational television talk shows that deliberately put their hosts in opposition to guests with extreme opinions and then involve the audience in the discussion. The hosts are typically right-wingers, and some go out of their way to be obnoxious and insulting. According to the *Daily News*, one confrotalk "has seen its verbose host [Morton Downey, Jr.] hauled off to court after slapping a guest."

congregate-care   *(adjective)*
Describing a growing type of retirement housing facilities, hotel-like developments that also provide health care for their residents.

Copper T   *(noun)*
Trademarked name for an intrauterine contraceptive device (IUD) manufactured by the Gynomed Pharmaceutical Company. Said to be safer and more effective than earlier IUDs, the new copper-clad T-shaped device was approved by the Food and Drug Administration for sale in 1988.

cosmoceutical   *(noun)*
A prescription cosmetic dispensed by a dermatologist to improve both the appearance and the health of the skin.

couch people   *(noun)*
Homeless people, forced by circumstances to sleep on friends' or relatives' couches.

Couch Potato™   *(noun)*
A person who prefers to spend his evenings relaxing before a television set. The term was coined by Robert Armstrong, a cartoonist who is promoting Couch Potato dolls and games, and who has founded a club to help spread his philosophy: "Watching TV is an indigenous American form of meditation."

coyote   *(verb)*
To send forest-fire fighters to rugged back country, where they may stay for days without relief.

cracker   *(noun)*
A computerist, or hacker, who uses his skills to break into computer security systems simply for his own amusement.

crackhead   *(noun)*
Slang term for a drug-user addicted to smoking crack, a highly addictive mixture of cocaine and baking soda in pellet form.

critical path   *(noun)*
A management technique, its name taken from science, that employs computers to determine the fastest and most efficient way to chart and control complex events.

cross-training   *(noun)*
An exercise system in which several sports—e.g., tennis, running, and swimming—are regularly practiced in order to produce balanced muscular development and generalized physical fitness.

cruciverbalist   *(noun)*
A devotee of or expert at crossword puzzles.

cryobirth   *(noun)*
The birth of an organism from a frozen embryo.

cryptomnesia   *(noun)*
Unconscious plagiarism of another's ideas—the unintentional borrowing of overheard words or concepts, presented as original thought.

crystal meth   *(noun)*
A powerful and popular illegal amphetamine. Produced in underground labs from ephedrine, red phosphorous, and hydriodic acid, crystal meth is highly volatile and explosive, but very profitable. The substance is said to be similar in effect to cocaine but cheaper and longer-lasting.

cyberpunk   *(noun)*
A high-tech computer technician with unconventional and extremely futuristic ideas.

D

D   *(noun)*
In basketball, D is short for defense.

Da Butt   *(noun)*
A dance craze inspired by Spike Lee's movie *School Daze*. *Newsweek* quotes a Chicago club host who explains: "Stick your butt out and keep moving to the music—then bend over and keep boppin'."

dancercize   *(noun)*
Conditioning exercise in the form of rhythmic dancing, usually in groups.

date-rape   *(noun)*
An assault in which a woman is coerced into sexual intercouse by an acquaintance or boyfriend.

dayparting   *(noun)*
TV programmers' term for the practice of pinpointing shows for particular audiences. Dayparting is based on market research indicating the time of day a targeted age or interest group is most likely to be seated in front of the tube.

Dazer™   *(noun)*
A battery-operated ultrasonic dog deterrent, now being tested by the U.S. Postal Service, that wards off menacing dogs with high-frequency sound.

D.B.   *(noun)*
Shortened form for the "drop-by," a Washington social ploy involving an arrival at a party, a quick shaking of hands, a circle of the room, and a speedy exit. The D.B., observed *The New York Times* in 1987, "is a fail-safe maneuver for the appearance that many feel they must make for business or political reasons or diplomatic courtesy."

Deadheads   *(noun)*
The name adopted by diehard fans of the rock-and-roll band Grateful Dead.

death-qualify   *(verb)*
To prevent opponents of the death penalty from serving on juries in capital cases.

deep pocket   *(noun)*
Legal slang for the party in a lawsuit with the most money. "The spouse with the assets—the 'deep pocket,' as he's known in the matrimonial trade—tries to divulge as little information as possible." (*New York* magazine)

def   *(adjective)*
Slang word for very good, cool, wonderful. Its origin is obscure—perhaps *definitely*—but "def" is being used to characterize anything from clothes to music; there is even a "Def" recording company.

DENK   *(noun)*
Acronym for dual employed, no kids—or childless working couple.

dense pack   *(noun)*
A system of MX missile-silo construction in tight clusters which, its supporters contend, would cause incoming enemy

missles to destroy one another before impacting and knocking out the MX installation.

designated drivers   *(noun)*
People who, at the beginning of an evening, agree not to drink and to take responsibility for driving home friends who have been drinking.

devastator   *(noun)*
An exploding small-caliber bullet brought to notoriety when used by John Hinckley in his assassination attempt on Ronald Reagan in 1981.

DEWK   *(noun)*
Abbreviation of dual employed, with kids—the more typical young family.

digit head   *(noun)*
Slang for a dedicated computer enthusiast.

dink   *(noun)*
Double income, no kids. Similar to a yuppie—trendy, upscale, and financially above average.

dis   *(verb)*
Street term meaning to show contempt for—shortened from disrespect.

dividend-capture   *(noun)*
An investment strategy that involves the purchase of high-yield stocks just before a company declares a dividend and holding them only long enough to get the payout.

DNA fingerprints   *(noun)*
Also known as "gene prints," the technique is based on the fact that everybody's DNA is unique, and that every cell in an individual has the same DNA. Therefore, examination of bloodstains, semen, etc., can be used for foolproof identification, even if the samples available are years old.

dockominium   *(noun)*
A marina in which boat owners buy their slips.

doc-watcher   *(noun)*
Informal term for an independent medical-review firm. With medical costs skyrocketing, employers and insurance companies are increasingly relying on doc-watchers to save them money by keeping track of patient-care costs and recommending the least expensive procedure for hospital cases.

dogolatry   dog-OLL-uh-tree   *(noun)*
The worship of dogs. Coined by newspaper columnist Colman McCarthy in 1987, "dogolatry" implies criticism of people who are more concerned with the luxurious life-styles of their pets than with the survival of their fellow human beings.

dope   *(adjective)*
Outstanding, superb, from *dope*, slang for drugs. "That's a *dope* Rolex."

dracontology   *(noun)*
Literally, the study of dragons. Currently referring to the inquiry into the possible existence of such improbable serpentlike creatures as the Loch Ness monster.

DRAMS   *(noun)*
Acronym for dynamic random access memory components.

dramedy   *(noun)*
Hollywood's name (drama + comedy) for a new genre of half-hour slice-of-life television shows that emphasize character and insight with a mixture of humor and gritty realism. Dramedies are generally shot on film instead of videotape, with only one camera and no laugh track.

DRIP   *(noun)*
Acronym for dividend reinvestment program, a plan allowing company shareholders to take their dividends in stock. Some companies issue stock for that purpose at a discount—in effect watering their stock.

drive-by   *(adjective)*
Pertaining to crimes committed from a moving vehicle, as in "drive-by murder."

dry beer   *(noun)*
A new and very popular type of beer, developed in Japan and recently introduced in America. Dry beer, which is less sweet than lager and has a higher alcoholic content, counters the recent trend toward "light" beers.

dry-season gardening   *(noun)*
A technique for producing crops in drought-stricken areas being promoted worldwide by UNICEF. The United Nations children's agency hopes the technique will help improve nutrition of youngsters in drought-plagued nations.

ducting   *(noun)*
An atmospheric condition that can affect radar signals. Ducting occurs when air strata of contrasting temperatures become layered together, forming a duct that can distort and bounce radar signals.

Dungeons and Dragons™   *(noun)*
A role-playing strategy game in which players with "magical powers" seek fortunes in a perilous maze of caverns guarded by mythical and occult monsters.

dustman   *(noun)*
An advocate of the theory that the planets of the solar system were created by the accretion of galactic dust in the sun's gravitational field.

DVP   *(noun)*
Abbreviation for Digital Voice Privacy network, an FBI national radio system designed to be secure from unauthorized listeners.

dwarf-throwing   *(noun)*
A controversial contest, probably originating in Australia as a competition between nightclub bouncers. In England it is a

show-business act where audience members vie to see who can pick up a dwarf (a professional entertainer) by the harness and throw him underhand the farthest into a pile of mattresses. Adverse public opinion is expected to stop the "sport."

E

ear candy   *(noun)*
Pleasing light music.

East Wind   *(noun)*
An intermediate-range ballistic missile made in China. A group of East Winds secretly installed by Saudi Arabia in 1986 was undetected by U.S. intelligence agencies until January 1988, whereupon the Saudis declared that the missiles would not be equipped with nuclear warheads or chemical weapons.

Ebonics   *(noun)*
(See *BEV*.)

Ecolyte™   *(noun)*
An experimental plastic wrapping material being developed by Ecoplastics of Toronto, it is photodegradable. Ecolyte used as a packaging would decompose under ultraviolet light (a component of sunlight) within a few months after use. Since UV light does not penetrate glass, however, Ecolyte-wrapped merchandise would be safe in store windows.

econobox   *(noun)*
An inexpensive small car, usually imported, that delivers basic transportation economically.

ecotage EK-oh-taj *(noun)*
A contraction of *eco*logy and sabo*tage*, ecotage is an extreme form of environmentalism. Dismayed by the widespread clearing of huge forest tracts, some activists have called for studding trees with nails to prevent sawing, and even for starting forest fires. "One of the best ways to foil the loggers," advises the radical environmental group Earth First!, "is to burn [the trees] down." The forests, says the group, "will recover much better than they will from clearcutting." Such tactics have been called "environmental terrorism" by lumber-company spokesmen.

ecstasy *(noun)*
A synthetic designer drug chemically related to both amphetamines and mescaline and said to produce a mild euphoria without the rush of cocaine, the high of cannabis, or the hallucinations and other unfortunate side effects of LSD. Despite its reputation in some circles as an aphrodisiac, the name "ecstasy" probably comes from its laboratory classification, "XTC." The DEA tried to have it classified with heroin and LSD as a controlled substance illegal for use for any purpose, but the courts have ruled it legal for experimental purposes.

ECU *(noun)*
Abbreviation for "extreme closeup," used in the motion-picture and television industry.

eldercare *(noun)*
A program offered by some corporations, eldercare is designed to aid employees burdened with the care of aging relatives.

electrofunk *(noun)*
Funk music played on electronically amplified instruments.

electronic cadavers *(noun)*
Computer-imaging techniques being designed so young medical students can "dissect" electronic images rather than use real cadavers for their initial lessons.

electronic cottage   *(noun)*
A worker's home when it is used as a computer-linked workplace. A homeworker in an electronic cottage (a spinoff from "cottage industry") is known as a computer commuter.

Energia   *(noun)*
The name of the U.S.S.R.'s unmanned booster rocket. At 198 feet, Energia is the world's largest launch vehicle, with a payload capacity of 220,000 pounds, nearly four times that of the U.S. space shuttle. According to *Insight*, "Energia can haul into orbit pieces of a second-generation space station, manned missions to the planets, or even the elements of a space-based defense against U.S. nuclear missiles."

energy return shoes   *(noun)*
Newly developed athletic shoes that are said to rebound more effectively so as to dissipate less of the wearer's energy when feet hit the pavement.

English creep   *(noun)*
The spread of English as an international language. *U.S. News and World Report* observed that "English has become to the modern world what Latin was to the ancients, dominating the planet as *the* medium of exchange in science, technology, commerce, tourism, diplomacy, and pop culture. So wide is its sweep that 345 million people use English as their first language and an additional 400 million as their second."

Enhanced 911   *(noun)*
An improved emergency-communication system being installed in cities across the country. By linking 911 phone calls to a data base containing all residents' names and addresses, the system instantaneously traces the call and displays its location for the emergency dispatcher even if the caller doesn't speak.

environmental theater   *(noun)*
A form of drama in which the audience interacts with the performers. Reviewing *Tamara*, a 1987 environmental theater offering, *The New York Times* observed that playgoers do not "sit

in seats but step inside a you-are-there representation of the Villa Il Vittoriale." Audience members, said the newspaper, then "choose an actor to follow from room to room. They experience the action and the villa through the life and eyes of that character." New Yorkers, noted the *Times*, had "mixed reactions" to the new theater format. Environmental theater productions are sometimes called "living movies."

ergometer   *(noun)*
A rowing machine with adjustable resistance that closely simulates water resistance; used for training rowing teams in the winter and for general exercise by fitness fans.

Etak Navigator™   *(noun)*
Trademarked name for an in-car electronic roadmap system designed by Californian Stanley K. Honey. Consisting of an electronic compass, a small trunk-mounted computer, a tape-memory unit, and a dashboard-mounted screen, the Etak shows the car's location on its lighted map with a green arrow.

ETS   *(noun)*
Abbreviation for environmental tobacco smoke. "Periodically," said the R.J. Reynolds Tobacco Company in an advertisement, "the public hears about an individual scientific study which claims to show that ETS may be harmful to nonsmokers."

Euromissile   *(noun)*
An intermediate-range missile deployed in Europe on both sides of the Iron Curtain.

Eurostyle   *(noun)*
A school of interior decorating that employs spare, dramatically colored furniture and accessories made from synthetic materials.

Eurotunnel   *(noun)*
A thirty-one-mile tunnel now under construction beneath the English Channel. Linking England and France, the tunnel is expected to be able to handle 2.3 million passengers and 5 million tons of freight a year. Also called the Chunnel.

evil empire   *(noun)*
An epithet used by Ronald Reagan to characterize the Soviet Union. The "evil empire approach" has come to mean an automatically hostile stance toward the U.S.S.R., which is held responsible for most of the world's problems.

F

facadism   *(noun)*
A compromise in city architecture whereby, as a concession to preservationists, the fronts of landmark buildings are retained as false fronts on entirely new structures. Developers are thus able to to build large new buildings by turning them into a sort of stage set.

facedness   *(noun)*
The tendency of one side or the other of the human face to be dominant. The study of facedness is relatively recent; early reports indicate, however, that in left-faced people, the left eye is lower than the right and the lines and dimples of the left side are the most distinct. One scientist, Dr. Karl Smith of the Univeristy of Wisconsin, says his research confirms that "all persons have a sort of facial fingerprint . . . just as they have distinctive patterns of left- or right-handedness."

factory farming   *(noun)*
The practice of raising such food animals as calves, hogs, and chickens in automated artificial environments that more closely resemble factories than traditional farms. Cost and profit considerations are paramount, and result in inhumane conditions, say *animals rights movement* advocates.

fast burn   *(noun)*
A system designed to reduce fuel consumption in gasoline engines through more rapid ignition, which increases the heat

and compression in the cylinder with a smaller amount of gasoline.

feeders *(noun)*
Animals raised to be eaten by other animals. Keepers in research laboratories and zoos feed mice and other small animals to reptiles without protest from animal-rights groups.

feemail *(noun)*
A derogatory Wall Street term for the legal fees generated by litigation settling "greenmail" disputes, which stem from shareholders protesting the ransoming of shares.

femmenism *(noun)*
The practice of feminism by men.

15-minute celebrity *(noun)*
A temporarily illustrious person whose renown fulfills the prediction of pop artist Andy Warhol "In the future, everyone will be world famous for fifteen minutes."

fifth force *(noun)*
A hypothetical force believed by some physicists to oppose gravity through short distances.

fifth-generation computer *(noun)*
A highly advanced robotic computer programmed with the ability to "think" and arrive at solutions to complex problems much as a human being would.

Filofax™ FY-low-fax *(noun)*
Trademarked name for a looseleaf pocket date book. The trendy, expensive (about $160 in 1988) five-by-seven-inch agenda book holds not only a day-by-day calendar but specialized inserts such as maps, bird-watchers' checklists, and pages for wine-tasting notes.

first-sale doctrine *(noun)*
A federal law permitting the purchaser of a product to resell or rent that product. First-sale doctrine was a widely heard phrase

in the recent controversy about the leasing of film cassettes by retailers; film studios went to court in an effort to halt such rentals, from which they received no royalties.

FIST   *(noun)*
Acronym for Federal Investigative Strike Team. Pooling the resources of law-enforcement groups at federal, state, and municipal levels, FIST operations are aimed at the capture of long-term fugitives wanted for major crimes.

fiver   *(noun)*
As a tither sets apart the tenth part of his personal income as a religious offering, a "fiver" allots five percent of his income or five hours of work a week for charitable service.

fixed mix   *(noun)*
A low-risk investment strategy in which a set percentage is invested in each of a variety of holdings. Annually, the mix is adjusted to maintain its original proportions by selling some of the holdings that have risen in value and buying more of those that have fallen.

Fjord   fyord   *(noun)*
A Norwegian breed of horse with dark tail and forelocks and horizontal stripes on its legs. Said to be descended from the steeds of the Vikings, the relatively rare Fjords have recently been imported to the United States, where breeders hope they will multiply.

flanker   *(noun)*
A companion product in a line of merchandise carrying the same brand name as the original item and designed to capitalize on the acceptance of an old familiar product but appealing to a different segment of the market. Ivory shampoo, for example, is a flanker of Ivory soap. Such spinoff products are also known to merchandisers as "line extensions."

Flashing™   *(noun)*
An electronic device developed in France that is said to eliminate the guesswork in selecting sexual partners. The pock-

et-size gadget, which is available in four wavelengths (identifying its owner as heterosexual, homosexual male or female, or interested in swapping partners), beeps when it comes within ten feet of someone carrying a Flashing tuned to the same frequency. If the person so contacted is not pleasing to the beholder, says the manufacturer, the machine can be switched off until its owner is out of range. "Le Flashing," first marketed in Paris, was introduced in the United States in Los Angeles.

flea flicker   *(noun)*
A razzle-dazzle football play wherein the quarterback hands the ball off to a running back, who in turn tosses it back to the quarterback who then throws it downfield to a receiver.

flex   *(adjective)*
Pertaining to personnel policies that allow employees to choose among a wide range of options in compensation, fringe benefits, and work schedules. Flex policies are said to save money and improve productivity on the one hand, and to provide employees with greater freedom to manage their jobs and families on the other.

flexible freeze   *(noun)*
An economic policy that permits overall spending to increase no faster than the rate of inflation.

flipper   *(noun)*
A money manager who specializes in initial public offerings (IPOs) of stock. Flippers (or "dolphins") buy stock in a new issue and sell as soon as the price rises.

fluffing out   *(noun phrase)*
A term used by some dedicated women executives to characterize less-determined colleagues whose lack of drive is reflected in soft, feminine clothing.

fluffy cellulose   *(noun)*
A flourlike food substance, made from bleached ground bran or citrus pulp and containing no calories or nutritive value. This

tasteless fiber is sometimes used as a flour substitute in low-calorie baked goods.

flugelwork *(noun)*
A new exercise system for fitness enthusiasts in which pool workouts are done with *flugeln,* inflated winglike attachments, on the arms and legs to increase water resistance.

fluoxetine *(noun)*
A new drug that shows promise of being an effective method of curbing overeating and alcohol abuse. Fluoxetine works by stimulating the release of appetite-suppressing natural chemicals in the brain.

flutter *(verb)*
To administer a lie-detector, or polygraph, test; from the test's measurements of a subject's nervousness, which may reveal guilt. Commenting on a large-scale test of the polygraph by the Defense Department, columnist William Safire referred to the device as "a modern instrument of mental torture" and asserted that "to force it on a suspect is to give him the fourth degree." The department, he continued, "can now flutter thousands of scared employees," which could "lead to the demand that tens of thousands of citizens submit to fluttering as a test of their patriotism."

flyover people *(noun)*
A television-industry term referring to the TV-viewing public living between the major production cities of New York and Los Angeles. Flyover people are presumed to be less sophisticated than industry insiders and therefore not likely to appreciate really intelligent programming.

focaccia foe-KOTCH-ee-uh *(noun)*
An increasingly popular, Italian-originated breadlike snack reminiscent of pizza. Made with yeast and usually herbs, focaccia dough is baked and then topped with tomatoes, onions, or mushrooms. Asked why focaccia's popularity has taken so much longer than pizza's, Italian food historian Giuliano Bugialli said, "Focaccia is a refinement. It's more avant garde."

focus group   *(noun)*
A panel of "typical people" questioned by market researchers
or pollsters in order to learn the reactions and feelings of those
questioned about subjects of interest to the questioners. Focus
group interviewees are frequently observed by researchers
through one-way mirrors.

Fortune 500   *(noun)*
A list of the leading U.S. industrial companies printed annually
in the business magazine *Fortune*, it has come to signify big
business in general.

401(k) plan   *(noun)*
A retirement plan offered to employees by some companies.
Similar to IRA and Keogh plans, the 401(k) allows employees
to contribute pretax dollars whose taxes are deferred until the
funds are withdrawn. These taxes may then be spread over ten
years. The plan permits depositors to withdraw money early
without penalties under hardship circumstances.

fourth degree   *(noun)*
Polygraph test. (See *flutter*.)

freezenik   *(noun)*
A supporter of a moratorium, or "freeze," on the manufacture
and use of nuclear weapons.

fresh   *(adjective)*
New, fashionable, though deemed passé by many rappers,
among whom it originated.

fresh-cell therapy   *(noun)*
The injection into the human body of a serum made from the
cells of freshly slaughtered animals. The highly controversial
rejuvenation treatment, alleged by its German practitioners to
restore youth, potency, and energy, has been called ineffective
and dangerous by many U.S. doctors.

frogmore stew   *(noun)*
A traditional dish from coastal South Carolina named for an extinct plantation. The stew's ingredients may vary according to the whim of the cook, but they usually include sausage, shrimp, corn, and spices, according to Verta Mae Smart-Grosvenor, author of *Vibration Cooking* (Ballantine Books, 1986).

front   *(verb)*
Rapper's term meaning to put up a front, dissemble.

front-end bra   *(noun)*
A vinyl cover, usually black, which is fitted to the front of an automobile to protect its finish from such road hazards as flying gravel and bug stains.

frontloading   *(noun)*
The practice, especially among legally underage college students, of quickly drinking a large amount of liquor before attending an event where no alcohol is to be served, or where drinking-age laws are strictly observed. Frontloading is considered a serious problem by many college administrators.

FSI   *(noun)*
Abbreviation for free standing insert, an advertisement placed with, but not printed in, a newspaper or magazine. FSIs typically consist of sheets of "money-saving" store coupons.

full-court press   *(noun)*
Originally a basketball term for a tactic in which the defending team harasses each member of the opposing team the entire length of the court, "full-court press" is now a political term as well. It is used in government circles to define a major lobbyist's campaign to influence lawmakers.

full field   *(noun)*
An FBI background check of a potential federal appointee. Short for "full field investigation," a full field involves a thorough examination of a candidate's habits, friends, memberships, and private as well as public activities.

fuzzword   *(noun)*
An apparently precise word that nevertheless confuses communication; elegant gobbledegook that gives the impression of clarity and sense while deliberately obfuscating. Sometimes fuzzwords, because of their frequent appearance in the nation's capital, are called "the language of the Potomac," an example of which is the government's use of "revenue enhancement" when it means "tax increase."

fuzzy sets   *(noun)*
A term used by psychologists for language so imprecise it causes confusion. Examples of such language are frequently found in warnings and instructions that can't be written in precise technical language, such as "squeeze firmly but not too hard."

F/X   *(noun)*
Motion picture and television shorthand for special effects; the optical or electronic distortions used by filmmakers to create images beyond the range of standard photography or recording techniques.

G

galaktobouriko guh-LAK-tuh-BOOR-eek-uh *(noun)*
A layered Greek pastry filled with semolina custard.

gamer *(noun)*
A player in football—and, occasionally, in other sports—known for playing the entire game full out regardless of injuries or setbacks; one who plays despite pain.

gamma knife *(noun)*
A device for treating brain abnormalities with gamma-ray beams rather than with surgical procedures. With the gamma knife, beams emitted from radioactive cobalt can be focused to intersect deep within the brain, where they perform such tasks as sealing ruptured blood vessels with a minimum of damage to other tissues.

gateway drug *(noun)*
A recreational mood-changing substance (e.g., marijuana) that is not medically classified as habit forming or potentially deadly but that may lead its users into experimentation with more potent substances, such as heroin.

gelcap JELL-kap *(noun)*
New one-piece oval-shaped pills that are easier to swallow because they are 33 percent smaller than comparable capsules.

These gelatin-coated medications are more difficult to tamper with because they do not come apart as readily as capsules.

gemfibrozil   *(noun)*
A widely used anticholesterol medicine that, while it lowers the cholesterol level only a little, effectively reduces heart attacks among those with elevated cholesterol levels. The drug works by altering the balance between the types of cholesterol in the bloodstream.

gene therapy   *(noun)*
The experimental technique of replacing a defective gene (the element that controls hereditary characteristics) with a laboratory-created gene; used in treating single-gene diseases, such as cystic fibrosis.

getaway special   *(noun)*
A small cargo payload carried aboard space shuttles. Two sizes of cylindrical container are available for rent from NASA (five and two- and-a-half cubic feet) for the transport into space of a great variety of experiments on the effects of weightlessness.

gimme cap   *(noun)*
An inexpensive baseball cap used as an advertising giveaway, usually brightly colored and decorated with the manufacturer's logo or name.

gîte   ZHEET   *(noun)*
French. A private country vacation home in France. One- to two-week rentals of gîtes are increasingly popular with vacationing Americans, who may thus occupy residences in areas such as Normandy, Brittany, the Loire Valley, and the French Mediterranean coast.

global commons   *(noun)*
Environmentalists' term for the total world ecological system of oceans, tropical forests, and the atmosphere.

gleaming the cube   *(noun)*
A skateboarding phrase for pushing oneself to the limit.

Glock 17   *(noun)*
A partly plastic, 9mm handgun manufactured in Austria for that nation's police and armed forces. Antigun groups oppose importation of the Glock, which they label the "Stealth bomber of the terrorist arsenal," on the ground that the weapon can easily evade detection by airport screening devices.

glowboy   *(noun)*
A nuclear-power plant employee who does maintenance work in the plant's dangerously radioactive areas, and who repairs equipment as quickly as possible to avoid overexposure to radiation.

Glycel™   *(noun)*
A "rejuvenating" line of skin-care products based on a patented ingredient called GSL, codeveloped and endorsed by Dr. Christiaan Barnard, the famed South African heart-transplant surgeon. The product is controversial because of its extravagant claims, and Barnard has been trying to distance himself from the association. "Like Gary Hart," he says, "I made a big mistake."

GM-CSF™   *(noun)*
A new drug that stimulates blood-cell production in patients with damaged bone marrow. GM-CSF (granulocy-macrophage colony-stimulating factor) was developed through genetic engineering by Immunex, an American biotechnology company, and has been used with promising results to treat radiation victims.

gnat-robot   *(noun)*
A micromachine under development that may soon be used for exploration and surgery inside the body.

go-go   *(noun)*
A U.S. military term for a government-owned and government-operated base, such as an arsenal, which has mostly civilian employees but is directed by army officers.

golden handcuffs   *(noun)*
A contract between a company and an incoming executive that guarantees the executive rewards that would be lost in the event of his or her leaving the company, thereby creating a financial incentive for loyalty. Sometimes called "diamond handcuffs."

golf-course effect   *(noun)*
The climate change, observed in such communities as Palm Springs, California, that occurs when desert areas are replaced by irrigated parks and golf courses. Over a period of fifteen years, the average temperature in Palm Springs has dropped three degrees through the evaporative effect of increased vegetation.

goo-goo   *(noun)*
Slang for good-government advocate. Speaking of Michael Dukakis, the 1988 Democractic presidential candidate, a friend said, "Michael is a Brookline goo-goo. That isn't all bad." (*Newsweek*)

golpe   GOLE-pay   *(noun)*
The sudden overthrow of a government; a coup d'état; the Spanish word for "blow" or "strike," golpe is generally used in connection with Latin American countries.

gomer   GO-mur   *(noun)*
Acronym for get out of my emergency room. Medical slang epithet for a patient with inappropriate requests or unsolvable problems who persistently applies for hospital treatment.

gorilla   *(noun)*
A block-busting film or record, in entertainment industry argot.

granola   *(noun)*
Updated word for "bohemian"; an individual whose life-style is earthy, unconventional, and self-designed. A granola, named for the rough-textured nut-and-grain food he or she often favors, is also—for the same reason—called a "crunchy chewy."

graphic novel   *(noun)*
A self-contained picture-and-word work that goes beyond the traditional thirty-two-page comic book and is helping to elevate the perception of comics as art. The most notable graphic novel, *The New York Times* reports, has been *Maus*, a memoir by Art Spiegelman, of Hitler's Germany, with line drawings and text that depict Jews as mice and Germans as cats.

greenfly   *(noun)*
The word means green peach aphid but has been adopted by professional baseball players to describe baseball groupies—those die-hard baseball fans who persist in hovering around player entrances and hotels, looking for a chance to hobnob with their idols.

green serpent   *(noun)*
A Russian nickname for vodka, whose excessive consumption is said to produce visions of emerald-colored serpents as well as pink elephants.

greenshoe   *(noun)*
The right of the general partner in a limited partnership to raise additional money without the legal requirement to issue a new prospectus. "The offering was capitalized at $50 million, with a greenshoe to $65 million" (from a letter from Ferris & Co. broker E.L. Johnson).

greyhound   *(noun)*
A very fast basketball player.

grip-and-grin   *(noun)*
Television news argot for a photo-opportunity occasion to be filmed or taped by a TV crew on Capitol Hill—a handshake among legislators and a smile for the camera.

grippers   *(noun)*
Elasticized bands of various sizes with metal clips at each end. Popular and fashionable, grippers are used to hold up leg warmers or pants, to pull in oversized jackets, or simply for decoration.

grok *(verb)*
Slang. To like or enjoy; "She really groks history."

group-bridging *(noun)*
An increasingly popular telephone service that makes group conversations possible. By dialing the number advertised, a customer can join a conversation with up to ten people, all of whom may be complete strangers. The charge for the call, billed on the customer's regular monthly statement, is typically about twenty cents for the first minute and fifteen cents for each additional minute.

G-7 *(noun)*
Abbreviation for Group of Seven, the international economic alliance of the United States, West Germany, Japan, Britain, France, Italy, and Canada.

guanxi gwan-shee *(noun)*
A Chinese word meaning connections, guanxi surfaces frequently in any transaction involving the Chinese, whether it is business, diplomacy or politics. Like the so-called old-boy networks in western countries, a network of personal connections—guanxi—is vital to the success of any enterprise in China.

Guardian Angels *(noun)*
A controversial group of young, unarmed, volunteer law enforcers who patrol the New York City subways and high-crime areas in some other cities. Popular with many subway riders, who say they feel safer with the "Angels" around, the group's members are considered by some law-enforcement professionals to be dangerous amateurs and vigilantes.

Gucci gauntlet *(noun)*
Washington, D.C., slang for the Capitol corridors where elegantly shod lobbyists congregate.

gynocriticism *(noun)*
The academic study of women's literature.

H

hair extension *(noun)*
The attachment of real or synthetic hairpieces to the head by a process that combines braiding, gluing, and burning.

happenin' *(adjective)*
Very good; stylish; the last word. "Hey, those are happenin' pants!"

Harold *(noun)*
A sport in which college- or company-sponsored teams, using techniques from improvisational theater, compete before an audience. Each team improvises a scene suggested by the audience, using word games, mime, songs, poetry, and dance but no scenery or props.

HDV *(noun)*
High definition video. A new process for converting video-taped productions to film. The transfer converts the tape's thirty pictures per second to twenty-four frames per second on film, causing the image to acquire such cinematic characteristics as grain and flicker and making it look like a standard motion picture. HDV pictures can be projected in theaters electronically and may be edited and revised at any time to respond to audience reaction.

heat-shock gene   *(noun)*
A gene that makes it possible for some organisms to survive intense heat. Biotechnologists hope to incorporate heat-shock genes, which occur naturally in some yeasts and in certain plants and animals, in commercial crops for hot climates.

heavy bead   *(noun)*
Pentagon budget jargon for the largest of the big-ticket items in the annual defense-budget request.

hell camp   *(noun)*
A rigorous Japanese leadership-training program scheduled to be introduced in the United States in 1988. In Japan, reported *Forbes* in late 1987, the thirteen-day program is "known as the management-training equivalent of Parris Island or Fort Benning boot camps. Leather lunged instructors chivy their charges through sixteen-hour days and endless repetitions of the proper way to write reports, deliver speeches, talk on the telephone, look after the health of subordinates, hammer out quick decisions." Hell camp directors assured U.S. business leaders that the system would "turn any manager you send into a knight in shining armor."

heptathlon   *(noun)*
An athletic contest of seven different track and field events in which the competitor who accumulates the highest combined score wins.

Herzog keyboard   *(noun)*
A new, patented computer keyboard designed to reduce stresses on the tendons and nerves of users' left hands. On the Herzog, the left-hand columns of keys extend diagonally upward to the right instead of to the left, a modification that, its inventors claim, will eliminate keyboard-produced carpal tunnel syndrome and tenosynovitis.

Hexapod   *(noun)*
A six-legged vehicle developed by Ohio State engineers to provide transport in rugged and marshy terrain that stops jeeps

and tanks. Controlled by computers connected to sensors, the ten-foot-tall machine is designed to travel at speeds up to eight mph.

hipo HY-poe *(noun)*
An employee, according to *The Wall Street Journal*, who is "on the fast track to success—someone with 'high potential.'"

hippo *(noun)*
An armored personnel carrier used by the South African police.

homeboy *(noun)*
From black English vernacular, homeboy is moving into the mainstream of widespread informal usage. The term originally referred to a member of the old gang in one's old neighborhood and is now sometimes used to mean "close friend."

homes *(noun)*
Short for *homeboy*.

hood *(noun)*
Street slang for neighborhood.

horchata *(noun)*
A popular Spanish drink made from a sweet-flavored root called chufa, horchata has been served chilled or frozen as a hot-weather thirst quencher since Moorish times.

hothousing *(noun)*
The trend toward the early educational stimulation of infants and toddlers—the "superbaby" phenomenon—the effects of which still remain to be proved.

house *(verb)*
From *bring the house down*. To have a major success, win great acclaim. "They *housed* the Apollo!"

HTR *(noun)*
Abbreviation for hard tissue replacement, a synthetic material said to reduce tooth loss in dental patients with periodontal

diseases. Researchers announced in early 1988 that the injection of HTR into areas of bone loss can cause the formation of new bone, thereby preventing teeth from loosening.

hubba   *(noun)*
A current street name for crack. "Jennifer, an 18-year-old transvestite, is smoking hubbas, or rocks of crack." (*Newsweek*)

Hummer™   *(noun)*
A new, high-mobility, multipurpose wheeled vehicle now in production for the U.S. armed forces. A one-and-a-quarter-ton payload machine of exceptional mobility and versatility, the Hummer is reported to handle off-road terrain with ease, climbing sixty-degree grades, fording rivers five feet deep, and conquering knee-high boulders. With different body configurations on one basic chassis, it fulfills many specialized functions—cargo/troop carrier, ambulance, or weapons carrier.

hummocks   *(noun)*
Street bumps that may be caused by hot weather, heavy traffic, poor quality asphalt, or buried steam pipes.

hush kit   *(noun)*
A muffler used to reduce excessive engine noise in jet aircraft. In order to comply with tough noise-abatement rules imposed by the Federal Aviation Administration, American aircraft manufacturers began to retrofit planes with the expensive (up to $3 million) new devices in late 1987.

hypercharge   *(noun)*
The force that makes objects fall at different rates depending on their chemical composition. The newly discovered hypercharge, some physicists contend, refutes Galileo's 300-year-old theory of gravitation, which states that all objects—from feathers to lead weights—fall at the same rate if they are dropped from the same height and if the effects of air resistance are discounted. If its existence is conclusively demonstrated, the hypercharge will be counted as the fifth basic force of the

universe. The others are gravity, electromagnetism, and the strong and weak forces that govern the structure of the atom.

hypertext   *(noun)*
Technology that gives computer users access to massive amounts of electronically stored information. One hypertext pioneer is the Perseus Project, developed by Harvard and Boston universities. In this program, reported *The New York Times* in late 1987, "Greek classics are being stored in computers, along with the English translations, commentaries, lexicons, and illustrations. A student coming across the name of an unfamiliar person or god in the *Iliad*, for instance, could immediately jump to biographical information about the character or to a painting of that character."

hypertriglyceridemia   hy-puhr-try-GLISS-uh-ride-EE-mee-uh   *(noun)*
A condition involving high levels of triglycerides in the bloodstream, which indicate increased risk of coronary disease.

I

illin *(adjective)*
Another word from black English vernacular, possibly deriving from "ailing" or "ill." Illin is gaining widespread usage with the verb "be," as a slang term for crazy: "You be illin, turning down a deal like that."

impitoyable ahm-pit-twa-YAHBL *(noun)*
A hand-blown wine-tasting glass shaped to emphasize taste and aroma. The word in French means "merciless" or "unsparing." The glasses are oversize to permit more oxygen to reach the wine when it is swirled, and have narrow mouths to concentrate the aroma. They are made in various specific shapes for different kinds of wine and are vital equipment for serious wine-tasters.

insider trading *(noun)*
The purchase or sale of a company's stock by an individual possessing nonpublic, special knowledge of the company's affairs. The Insider Trading Sanctions Act of 1984 makes such transactions a federal offense.

installation *(noun)*
Trendy term in the art world for "show." Originally referring to the placing of large sculptural works—which really needed to be "installed"—the term has come to mean any art presenta-

tion in a gallery or museum. Thus, an exhibit of paintings (an "installation") is no longer "hung," but "installed."

Intact Baby Movement   *(noun)*
A group opposing infant circumcision and seeking to persuade legislators in several states to pass laws requiring explicit advice to expectant parents regarding the pros and cons of the operation.

interactive toy   *(noun)*
A child's plaything designed to complement a movie or television series. One of the hottest items at the 1987 American International Toy Fair, reported *Advertising Age*, was Mattel Inc.'s Captain Power, "whose toy weaponry interacts with the tie-in syndicated and home video series *Captain Power & the Soldiers of the Future.*"

interiorization   *(noun)*
A process that preserves certain types of plants in their natural state for many years. Invented in Sweden in the late 1970s, interiorization was patented by the Weyerhauser Company of Tacoma, Washington, in 1986. The process, which involves the absorption of nontoxic chemicals, produces what are said to be "maintenance-free plants that look and feel lifelike" and that "last for years with only an occasional dusting."

intifada   inn-tuh-FAH-duh   *(noun)*
Arabic word for uprising. Intifada has come into widespread media use, generally referring to riots among Israel's Palestinian population.

intraluminal stent   *(noun)*
A toothpick-size device made of stainless steel mesh and designed to keep arteries open and blood flowing. Inserted into an artery on a balloon catheter, the stent is expanded against the wall of the artery and remains in place when the catheter is removed. In a matter of weeks tissue grows over the mesh, keeping the artery permanently open.

IRMA *(noun)*
Acronym for an individual retirement mortgage account in which money is borrowed in monthly installments from a lending institution that uses the borrower's house as collateral.

J

Jade Squad *(noun)*
Nickname for a New York City Police Department unit staffed by Oriental-American officers and assigned to combat Asian-directed crime syndicates.

January effect *(noun)*
Stock market term for the phenomenon occurring almost every year, when stocks that had been selling at depressed prices experience sudden rises. One explanation for the effect, says *The Value Line*, an investment survey, is that "investors often sell equities at a loss in December for tax purposes, beating them down to abnormally low levels in the process. Early in the new year these issues tend to rebound, often sharply, from their end-of-year lows." Although the January effect can "fail to materialize," says the newsletter, "it has occurred in most years in this century."

Jazzercise™ *(noun)*
A popular form of exercise performed to the beat of jazz music.

J-curve *(noun)*
An economic phenomenon pertaining to the relationship between dropping currency value and trade deficits. The J-curve shows, says financial reporter Peter Kilborn, "that after a country's currency falls, its trade deficit will grow a while before it shrinks. That's because a falling currency raises the

price of imported goods before customers can cut back on orders."

JOA   *(noun)*
Joint operating agreement—an arrangement under the Newspaper Preservation Act that allows competing newpapers to merge business operations when both papers are failing financially.

jib   *(noun)*
Acronym for the jack-in-the-box dummy used by CIA agents to confuse surveillants. The jib is popped up to replace an agent who has jumped from a vehicle, making it appear that the same number of passengers remain.

Joe Six-pack   *(noun)*
A term, thought to be coined by Soviet reporters, for the average American.

Joltmeter   *(noun)*
A device that measures the bumps and holes in a road. The Joltmeter was developed by the Automobile Association of America for a comparative study of highway roughness. A sensor installed in one of the wheels of a car transmits impulses to a receiver, which prints out a profile of the road surface.

just-in-time   *(noun)*
An innovative production-management and quality-control technique developed in Japan (where it is called *kanban*), which is coming into increasingly wide use in the United States. Just-in-time is based on minimum inventory, careful planning, and total quality control. It calls for the elimination of stockpiles of production parts and finished goods. All materials are in active use as part of work in progress, arriving just in time to be assembed into finished products, just in time to be sold. "Just-in-time makes manufacturing a competitve weapon," says *Forbes* magazine.

K

karaoke ka-rah-OH-keh *(noun)*
An electronic device from Japan that plays tapes providing a full backup for a lead singer. With a karaoke, an amateur vocalist can sing along with a professional musical background. Complete with a tape player, speaker, and microphone, it blends prerecorded music with the singer's effort.

key *(adjective)*
Very good, the best. "He plays key trumpet."

kick back *(verb)*
To calm down and cool off. Originally from street-gang lingo, "kick back" is moving into mainstream usage.

kiddie condo *(noun)*
A condominium bought by parents for their children to live in at college. This college housing is also a real-estate investment to help defray college expenses, if sold at a profit after graduation.

kidult *(noun)*
(1) A television-industry term for a viewer between the ages of twelve and thirty-four. (2) A composite of *kid* and *adult*, used to describe a person who is physically adult but whose interest in adult concerns, such as literature, expanded knowledge and

rational discussion, has never developed beyond the interests and capabilities of childhood.

Killer Egg   *(noun)*
A special-operations helicopter under development for the U.S. Marine Corps.

killer technology   *(noun)*
Innovative procedures so radical that they make an entire existing technology obsolete, as when the transistor replaced the vacuum tube.

krytron   *(noun)*
A high-speed timing device that may be used in the manufacture of nuclear weapons and in controlling nuclear detonations. The krytron is also used in the fields of oil exploration, standard weapons systems, and medical-equipment manufacturing.

kurogo   kuh-ROH-go   *(noun)*
Japanese word for traditional theater stagehands, who wear black clothing to render themselves invisible while changing scenes.

L

LA *(adjective)*
Abbreviation for light or low alcohol; usually applied to beer or wine.

la langue du Coca-Cola *(noun)*
A scoffing French term for the English language.

lamp *(verb)*
To take it easy, in hip-hop, or rap, slang, as in leaning against a lamppost.

lane block *(noun)*
A bowling alley practice in which a lane is more heavily oiled in its center than at its edges. Lane blocking, reported *The Wall Street Journal* in late 1987, "is designed to steer, or block balls toward the 1-3 pin 'pocket' whence most strikes spring. The object is to make customers happier by hyping their scores." Frowned on by the American Bowling Congress, lane blocks are enthusiastically defended by most bowling-alley proprietors.

laundromat-bar   *(noun)*
A combination restaurant, bar, and self-service laundry where customers may eat, drink, and socialize while their laundry is being done.

LBO   *(noun)*
Abbreviation for leveraged buyout, a transaction in which a small group of investors buys a company with largely borrowed funds. The debt is eventually repaid with income produced by the acquired company's operations or by the sale of its assets.

LD-50   *(noun)*
Abbreviation for lethal dose, 50 percent. A test used to measure the relative toxicity of household products, cosmetics, and drugs by finding the dosage level that kills 50 percent of a test group of laboratory animals. The commercial use of LD-50 has become a major target of animal-rights activists.

legs   *(noun)*
Staying power, usually used in referring to films. *"Scarface* broke out with a roar over the weekend, but some distributors are skeptical about the movie's legs" (*New York Post*).

lemon tart   *(noun)*
One of the many words coined by Tom Wolfe in his bestselling novel *The Bonfire of the Vanities*. A lemon tart is a type of woman frequently seen at high-society New York parties—"young, blond, and in the company of elderly moneybags" (*Newsweek*).

lexigram   *(noun)*
A geometric symbol devised by primate researchers who train chimpanzees to communicate by means of a special computer keyboard. Each key on the board carries the symbol for an object, action, or person—a blue triangle for "apple," for instance.

Libertad   *(noun)*
Mexico's new one-ounce silver coin. The Libertad contains one troy ounce of pure silver and is touted as the only general-circulation pure-silver coin that is legal tender.

LifeCard™   *(noun)*
A laser-encoded card introduced by Blue Cross/Blue Shield that makes it possible to have copies of complete medical records on a credit-card-size wallet card. As many as 800 pages of medical history, including X-rays, EKG, and even a personal photograph, will fit on one LifeCard. (See also *smart card*.)

life cast   *(noun)*
An increasingly popular art form, life casts are busts made from plaster molds taken directly from their subjects' faces.

lightsat   *(noun)*
A small *light*weight *sat*ellite designed to be placed in orbit with a rocket launched from high-flying aircraft.

limitchiki   limm-uh-CHEEK-ee   *(noun)*
Russian word for people with residence cards permitting them to live and work in Moscow for a limited time.

linear park   *(noun)*
A hiking, biking, and jogging trail converted from an old train route. (See *Rails-to-Trails Conservancy*.)

linear thinking   *(noun)*
A type of formal logic that, according to *New York Times* columnist William Safire, is "a brand of thinking that moves steadily from cause to effect to the next cause and so on."

liposuction   LIPE-oh-suk-shun   *(noun)*
A plastic surgery technique for removing subcutaneous fat cells. After a hollow tube called a cannula is inserted through a small incision in the skin, a high-powered vacuum pump sucks out the fat. Liposuction is used to remove unsightly bulges, not to treat obesity.

living fence   *(noun)*
A hedge that functions as a fence. Military and nuclear facilities are beginning to replace chain-link fences with four-foot-thick hedges of the Chinese trifoliate orange tree, which provides a more effective defense against intruders or terrorists. The orange tree forms a thickly intertwined mesh of tough branches bearing four-inch thorns and is almost impossible to cut through.

living movie   *(noun)*
(See *environmental theater*.)

lock-up-option   *(noun)*
A corporate move in which the subject company in a friendly takeover offers the acquiring company the right to buy some of its more valuable assets or additional equity in the company. Lock-up options make the company less attractive to other bidders but may also reduce the value of the stockholders' shares.

lollipop   *(noun)*
A condominium in New York City that takes its name from the general shape of the real estate involved. By law, condominiums must be built on some actual land, so some developers acquire "rights of way" in existing-building elevator shafts, together with legal title to the land under the shaft. The condo is then built as several new floors on the old building as surveyed. Then the condominium appears as an apartment building balanced, like a lollipop, on a long stem.

lookout block   *(noun)*
A trap play in football in which a blocker lets a defender go by, then yells "Look out!" before hitting him from the side.

lovastatin   *(noun)*
A new drug that cuts cholesterol levels by inhibiting the liver's production of cholesterol. Lovastatin can have adverse side effects on the liver and the eye lens, but with proper follow-up

care and a good diet, its effectiveness could make it the drug of choice in treating patients with elevated cholesterol levels.

lumen   LOO-men   *(noun)*
A food product made form soy protein that can be processed, it is said, into close imitations of real meat, including beef, chicken, ham, and sausage.

M

magalog   *(noun)*
A combination high-fasion *maga*zine and cat*alog*, often issued by a department store and sometimes carrying advertisements for merchandise not available in the store. Bloomingdale's catalog, for instance, carries full-page ads for cigarettes, which the store does not sell.

Maharam's Curve   *(noun)*
A statistical curve correlating exercise with mood. A study of "runners' high," conducted by Dr. Lewis G. Maharam, suggests that for each person there is a specific level of training that will create a better mood.

male bonding   *(noun)*
The formation of close personal relationships and loyalties among men.

mall rat, or mallie   *(noun)*
A young person who spends most of his or her leisure time hanging out with friends in shopping malls—eating, shopping, or just "making the scene."

mamou   *(noun)*
Slang for a thing, idea, or action that is really important or that contains overwhelming potential: the big mamou.

manga   *(noun)*
A new type of comic book, tremendously popular in Japan, that deals with every subject from erotica to sports, from politics to business. Manga account for 30 percent of the Japanese book market, and one, *Manga—Introduction to the Japanese Economy*, has been translated into English under the title of *Japan Inc.*

maquiladora   mah-KEEL-uh-dor-ah   *(noun)*
An American-owned factory in Mexico where products are assembled for U.S. distribution. Under the maquiladora program, U.S.-manufactured components are shipped south of the border, where they are put together by Mexican workers. This joint U.S.-Mexican program resulted from American companies' complaints that they could not successfully compete with foreign goods made with low-wage labor, coupled with need for jobs in Mexico. There are now about 1,000 maquiladora plants near the border, which employ hundreds of thousands of Mexicans.

Maranatha   mahr-uh-NATH-uh   *(noun)*
A member of the Maranatha Christian Church headquartered in Gainesville, Florida. Maranatha, in Greek and Aramaic Bibles, is an invocation: O Lord, come. The church, which exerts strong discipline over its members, combines evangelical, born-again Christianity with conservative political activism.

marital rape   *(noun)*
Forcible sexual intercourse within a marriage; recognized as a criminal act by courts of law during the mid-1980s.

Mark 3   *(noun)*
An experimental spacesuit designed by the Johnson Space Center in Houston. Aimed at giving its wearer greater protection from both "space junk"—man-made debris—and micrometeoroids, the Mark 3 is half metal, half fabric, and weighs more than 150 pounds. Like the all-aluminum AX-5 (See *tin man*), another new spacesuit model, the "zero prebreathe" Mark 3 would eliminate the procedure known as prebreathing. Designed to work at a pressure of eight pounds per square inch,

both the Mark 3 and the AX-5 would permit their wearers to suit up and step out of a spacecraft immediately. Wearing earlier models, astronauts had to prebreathe 100 percent oxygen for 3 1/2 hours to avoid getting the bends.

matures   *(noun)*
A new coinage for older Americans, "matures" is used by some market researchers who study the purchasing habits of various age groups.

maximinimalism   *(noun)*
An art movement that teaches that every small thing, when placed in a big thing, is art. In its catalog, the New York University art department observed that the maximinimalist school began when the French artist Sylvain Tati "made a small dot in the center of a [huge] canvas with a marker pen while crying, 'C'est l'art!'"

meatware   *(noun)*
Computer enthusiasts' slang for the human body.

mechatronics   *(noun)*
From *mecha*nics and elec*tronics*. The branch of engineering that seeks to synthesize computer and mechanical engineering and the automation of industry.

megadink   *(noun)*
Disdainful epithet used by older professional investment bankers for a conspicuous breed of younger colleagues, usually under thirty, who seem to enjoy being caricatures of "the Wall Street banker" in both clothing and manner.

mego   *(noun)*
Acronym for mine eyes glaze over. Used humorously, a mego is an event, performance, or piece of writing or art that produces dazed boredom in the observer. Also used adjectivally as in "the mego factor."

meltdown *(noun)*
A drastic deterioration or collapse of almost anything. Used originally to describe the melting of part of a nuclear-reactor core, meltdown has come into general useage. It was used almost universally in the media to characterize the 1987 stock market crash.

metalhead *(noun)*
A slang term for a heavy-metal rock fan, usually male and dressed in bizarre imitation of the admired musicians. Metalhead carries the implication that the so-named person is not very bright.

Mevacor™ *(noun)*
An anticholesterol drug from Merck and Company, considered to be a major advance in the field of cholesterol-lowering medicines when introduced in 1987.

micromachine *(noun)*
A tiny apparatus built by etching silicon chips with a photochemical process that produces cranks, gears, springs, and even turbines no larger in diameter than a human hair. Scientists believe that computer-guided micromachines will soon be able to perform surgical repairs within the body without the trauma of traditional surgery.

micromanagement *(noun)*
The detailed planning of localized operations by a central executive; most commonly used in the military when top commanders and civilian officials, usually apart from and prior to a military operation, set out minutely particularized orders that allow little or no decision- making by the officers on the scene of the action.

Micropacer™ *(noun)*
Trademarked name for a new running shoe from Adidas that incorporates a battery-powered, watch-sized computer in its tongue. The computer, connected to a sensor in the sole, flashes

a display that gives the distance, average speed, and elapsed time of a run.

MicroTrak™   *(noun)*
A diagnostic test for the detection of chlamydia, the most common veneral disease in the U.S., which strikes up to ten million Americans a year. *Time* magazine reports that "up to ten percent of all college students are afflicted with it."

MIDI   *(noun)*
Acronym for musical instrument digital interface, a technology that makes it possible to interconnect musical synthesizers, sequencers, drum machines, and personal computers, thereby allowing musicians to play on more than one keyboard simultaneously.

minidorm   *(noun)*
A house purchased by a college student's family to be operated by the student as a rooming house for other college kids. The minidorm thus provides its student-manager with both housing and an income for college expenses and the parents with an investment.

minimal miking   *(noun)*
A music-recording technique that attempts to reproduce the sound that would actually be heard by a member of a concert hall audience by radically reducing the number of microphones during the recording session. (See *multi-miking*).

mini-RPV   *(noun)*
An RPV is a remotely piloted vehicle. A mini-RPV is a small remote- controlled drone aircraft that carries a television camera and is used in combat reconnaissance.

ministorage   *(noun)*
A new type of self-service warehouse developed to accommodate the inhabitants of the condominium communities that have proliferated in the suburbs. These new homes don't usually have attics or basements for storage, resulting in great demand for places to keep unused family belongings.

Minitel *(noun)*
The terminal for the state-supported French videotex system, incorporating a keyboard, screen, and modem. Minitels enable users to tap a nationwide system of computerized data bases, both private and public. The terminals are installed free of charge by the state telephone service, and customers pay only for time spent on the system, which is charged on their monthly phone bills.

mirandize *(verb)*
Law-enforcement slang for reading a suspect his rights under the Supreme Court ruling (Miranda *v.* Arizona 1966) to remain silent and to have legal counsel.

MMDA *(noun)*
Abbreviation of money market deposit account.

MMIC *(noun)*
Acronym for monolithic microwave integrated circuit (pronounced mimic). Gallium-arsenide integrated circuits, which combine many components into a single computer chip, have been developed to replace silicon in high-speed electronics such as supercomputers and miniaturized radar systems.

mommy track *(noun)*
A new, so-called category of law firm associates who work with no prospects of advancement. Women who take advantage of growing benefits such as flexible working hours, child care, and lenient maternity leave find themselves left behind in career advancement.

monoammonium glutamate *(noun)*
A government-approved flavor enhancer developed as an alternative to MSG, monosodium glutamate. The Department of Agriculture says MAG has the same effect on flavor as MSG but without the sodium. Sufferers from "Chinese restaurant syndrome" will get no relief, however, as their sensitivity is to the glutamate, which is still present.

Monoclate   *(noun)*
A blood-clotting drug for treating the most common form of hemophilia, introduced in late 1987 by the Armour Pharmaceutical Company. Monoclate is a more concentrated treatment than has been available before, can be administered more quickly, and carries less risk of contamination by viruses.

monster man   *(noun)*
In football, a defensive back or linebacker who, having no set defensive assignment, roams the field in whichever direction the play dictates, gobbling up ball carriers and receivers.

motoball   *(noun)*
A popular sport in Europe but virtually unknown in America, motoball is a variety of soccer in which all the players except the goalie are mounted on motorcycles.

mooch   *(noun)*
Target of a commodity scam. In these frauds, telephone canvassers call hundreds of prospects in search of gullible victims, or "mooches," as they are known in the trade. When a potential "mooch" is located, a professional salesman, or "yacker," takes over to close the sale. Typical commodities involved in such scams are oil, gold, and diamonds; the frauds cheat consumers, typically older citizens, out of $1 billion a year.

moonwalk   *(noun)*
A dance step invented by Cab Calloway in which the dancer, by shifting weight from one foot to the other and gliding backward, produces the illusion of walking forward; Michael Jackson is celebrated for his performance of the moonwalk, which he popularized.

MOS bite   *(noun)*
The term used by television journalists for a man-on-the-street interview.

motherese   *(noun)*
Psychologists' term for the soothing, nonverbal language with which mothers communicate with small children. Some re-

searchers believe that motherese is cross-cultural, perhaps even universal, and that it is more an emotional bonding ritual than linguistic communication.

movideo   *(noun)*
Contraction of *movie* and *video*—a feature-length theatrical movie whose principal content is a rock-music concert or series of performances.

MPTP   *(noun)*
A synthetic-heroin street drug that produces symptoms closely resembling the stiffness and tremors of Parkinson's disease. Ironically, an outbreak of MPTP-induced Parkinson's in California has led to a breakthrough in medical knowledge and treatment of the disease, which afflicts many Americans.

MTSO   *(noun)*
Abbreviation for mobile telephone switching office, the central "switchboard" for a cellular mobile telephone system.

multimiking   *(noun)*
A music-recording technique that depends on a large number of microphones dispersed throughout the orchestra to pick up each section at close range. The resulting multiple sound tracks are then mixed electronically. (See *minimal miking*.)

muppie   *(noun)*
Acronym for middle-aged urban professional; a spinoff from yuppie. In Princeton, New Jersey, Mayor Barbara Sigmund decried what she called the "muppie invasion" of her town. "It's getting so you can't go to a luncheonette," she complained, "without having those damn plants hanging down in your face." Sigmund also noted that phenomena accompanying a muppie influx are what she called "terminal cutesification," "boutiqueification," and "bankification."

mushroom   *(noun)*
A hairstyle popularized by athletes, the mushroom leaves only a round or square mat of hair on top of the head. The rest of the head is clean-shaven.

N

NABCO *(noun)*
Acronym for the National Alliance of Breast Cancer Organizations, a nonprofit clearing house for the latest information on breast cancer and support groups.

naked short-selling *(verb)*
Wall Street jargon. In ordinary short-selling, the seller may "borrow" the stocks to sell to a buyer from a third party, "covering" that loan at some later point. In *naked* short-selling, the "borrowing" step is eliminated by broker-dealers, who may do this legally.

narcokleptocracy *(noun)*
A compound of *narco*tic, *klepto* (to steal), and *cracy* (a form of government), referring to the confederacy of drug dealers, military leaders, and politicians who conspire in drug trafficking to amass enormous profits, particularly in such Latin American countries as Bolivia.

NDE *(noun)*
Abbreviation for near-death experience, an event reportedly undergone by some people who have recovered from apparent death. Individuals claiming to have had an NDE frequently describe God, heaven, or other phenomena associated with the afterlife.

necklacing   *(noun)*
The practice in which black South Africans suspected of being opponents of the African National Congress are beaten by a mob of ANC members, or "comrades," and burned to death with a gasoline-filled rubber tire around their necks.

Neo-Geo   *(noun)*
A fashionable new "school" of art purporting to derive from postindustrial electronic society. Apparently abstract in appearance, Neo-Geo is claimed by its practitioners to represent the new reality, since life in the postindustrial world, they claim, is increasingly abstract in nature.

net-net   *(adjective)*
Final; the last word; the conclusion reached after all elements have been added and subtracted. "The net-net software picture, then, is a brighter one" (*New Haven Register*).

new age   *(adjective)*
Characteristic of the casting off of old traditional social values and attitudes in such movements as feminism, postindustrial art, and music.

new-age music   *(noun)*
Quiet instrumental music blending elements of jazz, soft rock, and classic music into an "easy-listening" and soothing sound that makes no demands on its listeners.

new-collar   *(adjective)*
New-collar workers are the middle class of the baby-boom generation; under the age of forty-five, with an annual income between $20,000 and $40,000, they form the backbone of the service industry. Formerly largely ignored, this broad section of middle America is coming under increased attention from business (for their multi-billion dollar spending power) and from political parties (as they represent 15 percent of the electorate).

nomenklatura   no-men-klah-TOOR-uh   *(noun)*
The secret personnel and job-description list in the Soviet
governing bureaucracy from which key people are selected for
new positions and advancement. The word is gaining wider
usage to describe the power elite in any country.

nopalitos   no-puh-LEET-ohs   *(noun)*
Leaves from the nopal cactus; popular in gourmet circles when
battered and deep-fried as "tempura Mexicana" or as a salad
ingredient.

NOPEC   *(noun)*
Non-OPEC (Organization of Petroleum Exporting Countries)
oil producers. Six NOPEC countries, Angola, China, Egypt,
Malaysia, Mexico, and Oman, cooperate on price and production levels among themselves and, to some extent, with OPEC.

norflaxin   *(noun)*
An antiobiotic developed in Japan that has proven to be almost
100 percent effective against penicillin-resistant gonorrhea. (See
quinolones.)

nori   *(noun)*
Paper-thin Japanese seaweed that is used to wrap the rice and
fish in sushi. Nori is grown on netting suspended from floats
and attains harvest size of ten inches long and one inch wide in
about forty-five days.

Notch Baby   *(noun)*
One of the seven million Americans born between 1917 and
1921 who retired and began receiving Social Security benefits
between 1982 and 1987. Because of careless wording, a 1972
congressional act, which was designed to guarantee that pen-
sion income would equal 42 percent of average wages, resulted
in giving post-1977 retirees benefits much higher than the rate
of inflation. Congress corrected its mistake by gradually phas-
ing out the excess rate for those who retired during the five-year
period (the "notch") between 1982 to 1987. It left, however, the
higher rate in effect for the 1977 to 1982 beneficiaries. Although

the Notch Babies' pensions are higher than the now rees-
tablished 42 percent rate because they retired during the transition, many formed a lobby to get back the higher rate being
paid to the earlier group, and tried hard to make it an issue in
the 1988 election campaign.

Nu-Trish a-B™   *(noun)*

Trademarked name for a new milk product that is claimed to
aid digestion. Similar to acidophilus milk but with added bacteria strains, Nu-Trish a-B is said to keep the digestive system
"balanced."

O

Oedipus *(noun)*
Acronym for the computerized *Oxford English Dictionary*, its last four letters standing for integration, proofing, and up-dating system. Familiarly known to its editors as Oedipus Lex, the entire sixteen-volume O.E.D. is being stored on three compact discs and will soon be available to the public.

oilgas'n'timber *(noun)*
Washington lobbyists' jargon for the industries favored by the Senate Finance Committee, which tends to leave the oil, gas, and timber interests alone when it comes to eliminating tax breaks. Oilgas'n'timber is spoken as one word in this usage.

oilspot *(noun)*
South African term for an especially volatile black community.

Old Crows *(noun)*
A society of electronic-warfare experts founded by retired U.S. Air Force major Bernie Zettl. Old Crow members, many of whom are former military or government procurement officials, often serve as weapons consultants to private industry. (See *beltway bandits*.)

Olestra™ *(noun)*
A new low-calorie, cholesterol-free fat substitute under study by the FDA as a food additive. Olestra tends to reduce existing

cholesterol levels and, because it passes through the body without being taken into the bloodstream, it reduces the possibility of side effects. Proctor and Gamble hopes this product will replace one third of the fats in shortening and cooking oil. Competing with Olestra is Simplesse™, a similar product made by the NutraSweet Company.

OliverShield™ *(noun)*
An adhesive-backed paper disc for protection against germs or foreign substances on public telephone receivers. The shields' ads warn customers to "stop making dirty phone calls."

omnicide *(noun)*
Literally, the killing of everything living, as in the hypothetical sterilization of the earth in a nuclear holocaust.

operateur op-ruh-TOOR *(noun)*
A business manager who emphasizes performance for price—providing better-performing products for a lower price through efficient management and sensitivity to customers' needs.

optical processor *(noun)*
A supercomputer now under development that is powered by light- transmitting gallium-arsenide chips instead of silicon circuitry. Optical computers will, according to their developers, be faster, lighter, and cheaper than comparable silicon processors.

Opus Dei *(noun)*
A Roman Catholic society. Opus Dei (Latin for "work of God") is dedicated to the goal of infusing religious significance into all phases of everyday life, asserting that God can be served without sacrificing one's normal life and livelihood.

orangemail *(noun)*
The out-of-court settlement that the producers of Agent Orange paid rather than face protracted litigation. Although available scientific evidence has not supported the claims of serious health problems caused by exposure to the chemical, manufac-

... or what? *(interjection)*
A slang expression of enthusiasm, "or what?" is the last phrase of a rhetorical question, of which the first part is implied. "Is that a great sunset, or what?"

overstride *(noun)*
In sports biomechanics, the counterproductive braking effect that occurs when a runner lengthens his stride with the lower leg so that each step jolts and slows the pace rather than increases it. (See *stride angle*.)

owl *(noun)*
One who believes that the greatest danger is not whether or not the arms race will provoke an attack, as the doves believe, or that U.S. weakness will do the same, according to the hawks, but that nuclear war might be unleashed through misunderstanding or miscalculation.

oxygen bar *(noun)*
A newly popular Japanese type of "bar" at which customers pay to breathe oxygen to reach a euphoric state. Oxygen may be inhaled in the bar at the rate of three minutes for a hundred yen, or may be rented by the tankful to be used at home.

ozone hole *(noun)*
A place in the earth's atmosphere where the ozone layer has been depleted, allowing higher than normal levels of ultraviolet radiation to reach the earth's surface. The greatest concentration of atmospheric ozone occurs at an altitude of about twelve miles, where it absorbs ultraviolet rays. Some scientists think that atmospheric pollution from industry, especially fluorocarbons, may seriously deplete the ozone, resulting in more harmful radiation and a warming of the atmosphere, which could melt the polar icecaps and cause worldwide coastal flooding.

P

packwood *(verb)*
A word enjoying widespread use in Washington, meaning to reverse one's field, legislatively speaking. It has its origin in the propensity of Senator Bob Packwood (R-OR.) for drastically changing his position on issues. "I think the senator will packwood on the Saudi arms sale."

Pac-Man defense *(noun)*
In corporate-takeover parlance, the strategy named after the video game in which the target company turns and attempts to swallow its attacker.

paint *(verb)*
In electronic warfare, to lock onto a target with air or surface radar.

Pamyat *(noun)*
A Russian nationalist organization (*pamyat* means "memory") founded in 1980 to prevent destruction of Moscow's historical and cultural monuments. In 1987 the Soviet press exposed this group for its growing, virulent anti-Semitism.

Panda *(noun)*
China's one-ounce gold bullion coin, which has acquired numismatic value because its design and date are changed every year.

panto   *(noun)*
In British theatrical tradition, a production combining vaudeville, satire, and music.

parallel processing   *(noun)*
A new computer technology that solves problems more quickly by the use of multiple processors operating together under the direction of a mainframe computer.

pathography   *(noun)*
A growing literary genre named and defined by Joyce Carol Oates. By her definition, the form's motifs are "dysfunction and disaster, alcoholism and breakdown and outrageous conduct." Recent examples are cited: Albert Goldman's *The Lives of John Lennon* and *Elvis* and *Picasso* by Arianna Stassinopoulos Huffington.

Pavulon   PAV-you-lon   *(noun)*
A drug that induces muscle paralysis; used by anesthetists in some forms of surgery.

pay-per-transaction   *(noun)*
Also known as p-p-t, pay-per-transaction is an arrangement in which videocassette-rental stores agree to pay royalties on the rental revenue of a tape to the owner of the film rights. In return, the stores are allowed to buy the tapes for a fraction of their normal price, enabling them to stock more popular films.

peewee tech   *(noun)*
Abbreviation for "peewee technology"—small companies in the telecommunications or computer-related industries.

Pelli-Robson Chart   *(noun)*
A new eye chart designed to help optometrists and ophthalmologists pinpoint vision problems and early signs of eye disease. In testing at the National Eye Institute, the chart contains letters of equal size that become progressively lighter toward the bottom of the chart, eventually nearly disappearing.

penne   *(noun)*
Tubular pasta cut diagonally at each end, like a penpoint, hence the name, which means "pen" in Italian.

people meter   *(noun)*
A device designed to measure TV audiences more accurately and quickly than the present Neilsen ratings, which depend on household meters and diaries. People meters employ a remote handset with eight numbered buttons, each assigned to a household member, who presses the designated button when he starts to watch TV and when he stops. The meters, therefore, can measure not only how many people watch any show but what kind of audience they are, as well as monitoring VCR usage and the amount of zapping that occurs.

peredishka   perra-DISH-kuh   *(noun)*
Russian for "breathing space." Speaking of Mikhail Gorbachev's Third World retrenchment, former president Richard Nixon said, "This is an argument that says they need *peredishka*, or a respite, for the next ten years." (*Insight*)

perestroika   purr-ess-TROY-kuh   *(noun)*
Russian for "restructuring." The word is used by Soviet leader Mikhail Gorbachev to describe his new economic reform, which attempts to decentralize and "democratize" the Soviet system.

Peter Pan syndrome   *(noun)*
Pop psychology term for the personality disorder that characterizes men who are emotionally childlike throughout their lives.

petracide   *(noun)*
The destruction of ancient historic stonework, as when bombs and artillery caused heavy damage to Angkor Wat in Cambodia during the Vietnam War or when, in 1985, terrorist bombs defaced Borobudur, a treasured Buddhist temple in Indonesia.

P4   *(noun)*
Technically, a polymer called polyacrylamide that has improved greatly the efforts to keep soil properly moist. P4 sucks

up water like a sponge, then slowly releases up to 95 percent of its moisture to the roots of thirsty plants.

Phoenix heart   *(noun)*
An artificial heart developed by a U.S. dentist, Dr. Kevin Kuo-tsai Cheng, independent of any major artificial-heart institutions. Although it had been tested only twice in calves for periods of four and twelve hours, the Phoenix heart performed perfectly for eleven hours in an emergency human heart-transplant operation.

photocard   *(noun)*
A greeting card with a family snapshot and a message, which, with the recent spread of minilabs in the photodevelopment business, can be printed as easily and quickly as standard pictures.

phreaking   *(noun)*
Computerists' slang for the procedure by which hackers gain illegal use of telephone companies' long-distance services.

pick it   *(verb)*
To field well in baseball. A player who consistently makes good plays is said to be able to pick it, as in "Fred can really pick it at third base."

pinheads   *(noun)*
Self-adopted nickname for collectors of Olympic souvenir pins. Each Olympics spawns many different designs of pins, commemorating the various events and publicizing sponsors. Valued as collectibles, these pins are traded by pinheads nationwide.

pink collar   *(adjective)*
Pertaining to lower-level workers in offices and banks, etc., and usually referring to women. Pink collars are a cut below white collars.

pink sheets   *(noun)*
The National Quotation Bureau's daily list of stock prices, named after the pink paper on which it is printed. The pink sheets list companies whose public shares are too small to be carried on the New York or American stock exchanges or even governed by the SEC.

PIP   *(noun)*
Acronym for picture in picture. In digital TV sets, the simultaneous display of a second picture in the corner of the screen. The PIP permits monitoring what is being recorded on a VCR or the picture from a closed-circuit camera somewhere else in the area.

playfood   *(noun)*
Plastic replicas of popular food products. Such major food chains as Burger King and Pizza Hut have entered licensing agreements with toy manufacturers to produce copies of some of their well-known offerings. Realistic-looking pizzas and Whoppers, complete with fries, lettuce, tomato, pickles, cheese, onions, and the box they come in, have become hot-selling toys.

playtza   *(noun)*
A conditioning and relaxing therapy said to have originated in Bulgaria. In playtza the subject is gently whipped with oak leaves prior to a steam bath and/or sauna.

plyometrics   *(noun)*
A conditioning program designed to improve strength and endurance, plyometrics involves exercising with small, pliable balls weighing from 2 to 16 pounds.

poco   *(adjective)*
Short for "*politically correct*"; often used by feminists to describe nonsexist language.

podmall   *(noun)*
Also known as a convenience center, the podmall is a small shopping center with a few small stores and a small parking lot. It answers basic shopping needs in densely populated urban

areas whose large shopping centers have moved out into the suburbs.

pods *(noun)*
Derogatory slang from the computer world for corporate employees who closely resemble one another in style and behavior.

point guard *(noun)*
In basketball, the player charged with running the offense and, whenever possible, with handling the ball. The team's other guard, designated the off guard or shooting guard, is often a better shooter but a less adept ball handler.

pool reporter *(noun)*
One member of a large group of journalists who is selected to cover a meeting or other event barred to the group as a whole. The pool reporter shares the information he gathers with his or her colleagues in return for the right to witness the event in question.

populuxe *(adjective)*
A portmanteau word (popular + luxury), coined by Thomas Hine, design critic for *The Philadelphia Inquirer*, to characterize the decade after the mid-50s when conspicuous consumption coincided with vulgar design to produce a decade of kitsch.

portfolio insurance *(noun)*
A strategy employed by large investment houses to protect their own and their clients' portfolios against fluctuations in the market caused by computer *program trading*.

posse PASS-ee *(noun)*
A Jamaican teenage criminal gang. Originating in the ghettos of Kingston, Jamaica, and dealing mainly with marijuana, posses are now widespread in New York and have expanded to dominate the crack market and gunrunning in that city.

pothole politician   *(noun)*
An unflamboyant elected official who maintains his or her popularity by concentrating on such voter priorities as street repair and sanitation.

pour   *(noun)*
A press party where drinks are served. "New York media types are getting invites to a *real* pour for a change." (*Variety*)

power breakfast   *(noun)*
A morning meeting at which business is transacted over coffee and eggs, especially popular with advertising executives and entertainment-industry moguls.

practical shooting   *(noun)*
A sport based on the armed-combat courses used for years to train police officers under simulated dangerous conditions, with lifelike silhouettes of armed "bad guys" appearing suddenly along the course. Competitors, who use real bullets, are scored on their ability to hit in a "kill zone" and are penalized for shooting "innocent bystanders."

praisery   *(noun)*
Informal term for a public relations organization.

precip   PREE-sip   *(noun)*
Shortened form of precipitation now widely used by TV weather forecasters. According to columnist Russell Baker, this usage runs against the rule that polysyllabic words tend to replace simple ones in broadcasting. "Here we have a big word, 'precipitation,' that drove out a little word, 'rain,' now being shrunk to a breezy short word—'precip.'" (*The New York Times*)

preem   *(noun)*
A premiere performance or showing. "Jan Schutte's German film *Dragon Chow* has its U.S. preem May 27 at Lincoln Cinemas." (*Variety*) *Preem* is also used as a verb—to introduce.

pregaphone   *(noun)*
A device resembling a small megaphone or speaking tube, used by expectant mothers to speak to their unborn children. According to René Van de Carr, a California obstetrician who endorses the pregaphone, fetuses can be taught to understand what is going on outside the womb. The pregaphone is for mothers-to-be; expectant fathers can just bend down and talk.

price-sales ratio   *(noun)*
A tool used by stock market analysts to measure prices against sales rather than against earnings (the price-earnings ratio) as a technique for selecting stocks.

program trading   *(noun)*
A strategy of using computer programs to monitor the price differences between stock index futures in the Chicago exchanges and the market price on the New York Stock Exchange. When the price of futures rises, computer-generated trading automatically sells futures and buys stock or vice-versa when stocks rise above futures. Some analysts think that massive computer selling gave impetus to the '87 market crash.

progun   *(adjective)*
Adhering to the right of all citizens to bear arms; the opposite of gun control. A progun candidate for office might be favored by such groups as the National Rifle Association or the John Birch Society.

promenade theater   *(noun)*
(See *environmental theater*.)

Prop Art   *(noun)*
Short for propaganda masquerading as art. In *The New York Observer*, art critic Hilton Kramer wrote, "what is nowadays packaged and promoted and merchandized and even written about as art isn't really art at all but a species of political and cultural propaganda masquerading as art."

prosumer   *(noun)*
As predicted by Alvin Toffler, prosumers will be older people who will continue productive life for the good of their families and friends, by producing goods and services voluntarily and without financial compensation.

PSI   *(noun)*
Abbreviation for Pollution Standard Index, a system used by the Environmental Protection Agency to measure the quality of the air. On a scale of 0 to 500, 0 to 50 is good, over 100 is unhealthy, and above 200 is hazardous.

PT boat   *(noun)*
In basketball, a small, quick guard.

pubcaster   *(noun)*
Journalese for *pub*lic broad*cast*ing station, radio or TV.

puddle   *(noun)*
A subsection of a company's inventory, usually containing only one of the product types included in the company's overall inventory, or "pool."

Q

QFIA *(noun)*
Quantitative fluorescence image analysis—a diagnostic test for the early detection of bladder cancer. QFIA uses a fluorescent dye that adheres to DNA molecules (present in significantly higher concentration in cancer cells) and makes them clearly visible under a microscope.

quant *(noun)*
A stock market "whiz kid" analyst. Quants were named for their quantitative mathematical methods.

quartz-halogen lamp *(noun)*
An incandescent light fixture whose quartz bulb contains halogen gas and a tungsten filament; widely used for car headlights and other applications requiring brilliant illumination. The filament burns more intensely than those in ordinary bulbs and therefore produces a brighter and whiter light; the lamp also has a longer life than other bulbs because the vaporized tungsten reacts with the halogen and is redeposited on the filament, constantly renewing it and preventing blackening of the bulb.

Quick Snap™ *(noun)*
A disposable 35-mm camera introduced by Fuji. Quick Snap comes "preloaded"; after the film is shot, the whole camera is sent for developing.

quinolones   KWIN-a-lones   *(noun)*
A class of synthetic antibiotics that are effective against penicil-lin-resistant bacteria, which they kill by destroying the bacteria's DNA. Because the quinolones can usually be ad-ministered orally, they can reduce medical expense by helping eliminate the long hospital stays often required by intravenous treatments.

R

radical   *(adjective)*
Surfer slang for incredible, awesome.

Radio Marti   *(noun)*
A broadcasting service authorized by Congress to transmit a mix of daily radio programming, including propaganda, news, music, features, and sports, to Cuba. The service, named for Cuban patriot and writer José Martí, broadcasts as a division of the Voice of America.

radon daughters   *(noun)*
Radioactive particles present in tobacco smoke which, smoking opponents claim, may imperil the health of nonsmokers.

rai   rye   *(noun)*
A type of music popular in northern Africa, characterized in *People* magazine as "space-age Arabian folk music."

Rails-to-Trails Conservancy   *(noun)*
A group formed in Washington, D.C., to help civic organizations around the country take over abandoned railway rights-of-way and convert them to trails for bicyclists and hikers. According to *U.S. News and World Report*, the conservancy's eventual goal is "one long network of *linear parks* stretching from the Atlantic to the Pacific."

Rainbow   *(noun)*
A member of the Rainbow Family of Living Light, a loose
national confederation of unreconstructed hippies from the
1960s and other like-minded, back-to-nature, people. Rainbows
get together every year, 20,000 strong, for a week-long camp
meeting in one of the national parks—an event not always
enthusiastically welcomed by locals and park rangers.

rain insurance   *(noun)*
A policy issued by some underwriters to compensate
vacationers for hotel and travel costs incurred during periods
of rain or other inclement weather.

ranchera   ran-CHAIR-uh   *(noun)*
Spanish-style country and western music.

Reaganaut   *(noun)*
An ardent supporter of the policies of Ronald Reagan.
("Reaganite" is also used to describe such a supporter.)

red-bag waste   *(noun)*
Infected trash from hospitals that is supposed to be packaged
in special red bags, which are then sterilized or incinerated.

rehaber   REE-hab-ur   *(noun)*
A member of one of several groups dedicated to wildlife preservation, who cares for injured or orphaned animals until they
can be returned to the wild. There are two thousand licensed
(by state and federal wildlife agencies) rehabers in the United
States.

resource recovery   *(noun)*
The most recent designation for *trash-to-energy* technology.

retrorunning   *(noun)*
The sport of running backwards. One hundred and thirty-five
retrorunners competed in the Backwards Mile Race in New
York City's Battery Park in the spring of 1988.

Revenger   *(noun)*
An adult toy from Express Yourself, Inc., in Charlotte, N.C., which attaches to the dashboard of a car and simulates war sounds. The radar detector-size gadget has buttons for grenade, machine-gun, and death-ray noises with accompanying flashing lights; by pushing a button, the driver can "revenge" himself harmlessly on other motorists.

Rhino   *(noun)*
An acronym used in the British school system for a student who is *r*eally *h*ere *i*n *n*ame *o*nly.

ribbon speaker   *(noun)*
An extremely high-fidelity speaker that consists of ribbons of very thin aluminum foil. Its woofer is twelve inches wide and over six feet high, with the midrange and tweeters correspondingly narrowing down to less than one-quarter inch. Through a complex technology, they are said to produce vibration-free sound unmatched by any other type of speaker.

right tail   *(noun)*
Section of a statistical curve of desirable characteristics into which the "ideal" applicant to an elite university would fall.

riot shield   *(noun)*
A resilient and lightweight screen carried by police officers in self-defense against armed members of a hostile crowd.

river riding   *(noun)*
The sport of driving a jeep or other all-terrain vehicle through the water in the bed of a shallow river.

rocket docket   *(noun)*
The admiring epithet being applied to the federal courts of the Eastern District of Virginia, which are said to be setting new standards for fairness, consistency, speed, and efficiency. The national average for elapsed time between the filing of papers in a civil trial and the start of the trial is fourteen months; in the rocket docket, it's five months.

rocket scientist   *(noun)*
Originally a math- and computer-trained finance whiz on Wall Street (See *quant*), rocket scientist is coming into general informal usage to describe a bright, intelligent person. "Jane is a charming young lady, but she's no rocket scientist."

rock jock   *(noun)*
A mountain-climbing enthusiast, especially one who does serious technical rock climbing.

rockplowing   *(noun)*
The conversion of upland seasonal wetlands into farmland. In rockplowing, rock outcrops are pulverized into rubble, which is used to level the land for crop planting in the dry season. Environmentalists protest the process, claiming it destroys areas that function as water purifiers and wildlife habitats.

rollover   *(noun)*
An accident in which a motor vehicle rolls over. The National Highway Traffic Safety Administration is considering setting federal rollover standards and studying charges that Jeeps and similar vehicles tip over too easily.

rubber mirror   *(noun)*
A mirror, actually made of glass, used to eliminate the "twinkling" of stars caused by the rippling effect of atmospheric heat. The distorted light is reflected from the mirror through a telescope, which straightens out the image so that it can be photographed.

run-and-gun team   *(noun)*
A basketball team whose principal strength lies in fast running and accurate shooting ("gunning").

runza   RUN-zuh   *(noun)*
A traditional and popular food item in Nebraska, runza is an oblong pastry filled with beef, cabbage, and onions.

S

sakau *(noun)*
A nonalcoholic but intoxicating Polynesian drink made from the root of the pepper plant. Popular in Polynesia for thousands of years for its soothing narcotic effect, sakau is about to be introduced in the United States, although there is some question whether the bitter, earthy flavor will appeal to American palates.

salaryman *(noun)*
Japanese white-collar worker and junior executive.

samogon suh-MUH-gyon *(noun)*
Homemade vodka in the U.S.S.R. The campaign against drinking initiated by Mikhail Gorbachev has reduced the supply of legal vodka and driven its prices up drastically, causing a boom in *samogon* distilling.

sanctuary movement *(noun)*
An informal association of United States citizens, most of them members or leaders of churches and synagogues, who help refugees from wartorn and oppressive Central American countries enter the U.S. or Canada. Some movement members have been arrested and charged with violating immigration laws.

sandwich generation   *(noun)*
The group of Americans who find themselves responsible for both their parents' and their children's welfare. With the number of people over sixty-five increasing, more adults are having to cope with their elderly parents moving in while they are still raising their own children. (See also *boomerang*.)

sandwich music   *(noun)*
A blend of jazz and rock music.

sanguinarine   sang-GWIN-uh-reen   *(noun)*
A plaque-fighting compound in a new toothpaste and mouthwash that not only removes dental plaque but stops its growth. Sanguinarine, which comes from the bloodroot plant, has been used for years in folk medicine, but its effectiveness against the bacteria that cause plaque was only recently discovered.

Santeria   San-teh-REE-ah   *(noun)*
The polytheistic religion brought to the West Indies from Africa by slaves in the eighteenth century, and into the U.S. more recently with the influx of Caribbean immigrants. Animal sacrifice and "possession" rituals, in which participants become inhabited by gods, are integral parts of Santeria.

Saum   sawm   *(noun)*
Islam's holy month of fasting, during which all healthy Islamic men must abstain from food, drink, and sex from dawn to sunset.

scorched earth   *(noun)*
On the battlefield of corporate takeovers, a self-destructive strategy designed to make the target company less attractive to its assailants, perhaps by disposing of desirable assets or divisions or by arranging for all its debts to come due at once in the event of a takeover.

screwdriver plant   *(noun)*
Informal term in industry for a factory that assembles finished products from components produced elsewhere.

script writer   *(noun)*
A doctor who illegally sells prescriptions for pain-killers, stimulants, and depressants for recreational use, sometimes operating under the cover of a "diet" or "stress" clinic.

SEALS   *(noun)*
Acronym for Sea-Air-and-Land-Soldiers, the U.S. Navy's elite and secretive special-operations force. The SEALS are expert at underwater demolition and reconnaissance.

Seaspeak   *(noun)*
A new, English-language, internationally used set of maritime terms that may, according to *U.S. News and World Report,* "become the official language of shipping."

Seattle Foot™   *(noun)*
A prosthetic device that allows amputees to walk and run with close to normal action. With a sculptured polyurethane exterior and a plastic shock-absorbing spring in the heel, it looks and acts like a real foot, with the heel providing thrust as the spring releases its stored energy.

Sea Wing   *(noun)*
A high-tech swim fin devised by Scubapro of Rancho Dominguez, California. Resembling an airplane wing, the Sea Wing develops lift and thrust from the unequal pressure of water flowing across its surfaces. Vents that open and close with the swimmer's stroke create higher pressure on the upswing and lower on the down.

secondhand smoke   *(noun)*
Exhaled smoke from another's cigarette, cigar, or pipe; also called *ETS* (environmental tobacco smoke), or *sidestream smoke.*

securitization   *(noun)*
A new buzzword in financial markets for publicly sold issues of asset- backed securities. Automobile loans and computer-lease receivables, for example, are packaged and sold as securities.

Sgr A*   *(noun)*
An object near the center of the Milky Way galaxy that radiates enormous amounts of energy. Sgr A* is an ellipse one billion miles wide by almost two billion miles long, relatively small on the galactic scale and in relation to its energy output. Scientists suspect from its behavior that it is the accretion disc around a black hole.

shakuhachi   shak-uh-HAH-chee   *(noun)*
The Japanese bamboo flute on which music for Zen meditation is played.

shank   *(verb)*
To stab, in street-gang argot.

shapesuit   *(noun)*
A women's one-piece garment made of lightweight elastic material; not unlike what used to be called a corset, a word that, like girdle, has virtually disappeared from the language of fashion.

shareware   *(noun)*
Noncommercial computer programs distributed inexpensively through user groups or software libraries.

shark repellent   *(noun)*
Measures taken by a company to ward off a threatening ac-quirer, or shark, in a takeover conflict.

shock jock   *(noun)*
A radio disc jockey who tries to outrage listeners by sprinkling his show with profanity.

short-swing rule   *(noun)*
An SEC law that prohibits insiders from profiting by buying their company's stock low and selling high within six months, or from first selling high and then buying low.

shot clock   *(noun)*
A 45-second clock now used in all National Collegiate Athletic Association games. The clock gives a team up to 45 seconds to attempt a field goal, after which it loses possession. The new system is designed to prevent teams from maintaining possession indefinitely, especially in trying to hold a lead late in a game.

Showscan™   *(noun)*
A process developed by Douglas Trumbull, noted for his special effects in *2001: A Space Odyssey,* to bring brighter, more lifelike pictures to the movie screen. The 35-millimeter film introduced by Edison in 1890 and the 24 frames-per-second filming standard, which began in the twenties, would be replaced by 70-millimeter film photographed and projected at 60 frames per second. While acknowledging the superior quality of the new process, the film industry has been slow to commit itself because of the expense involved.

shredders   *(noun)*
Riders of short, highly maneuverable surfboards, known for their hotdogging style.

shred   *(verb)*
In surfer's slang, to perform a kicking swing at the top of a wave that throws up a sheet of spray.

shurocracy   shoo-ROCK-ruh-see   *(noun)*
A term coined by the late President Mohammed Zia-ul-Haq of Pakistan to characterize his regime and give it a democratic veneer, shurocracy comes from the Arabic *shura,* meaning advice or consensus.

sick building   *(noun)*
An office building whose inadequate ventilation forces employees to breathe recycled air contaminated with chemicals and disease- producing microbes. Workers in such buildings report significantly higher incidence of illness than normal.

sidestream smoke   *(noun)*
(See *secondhand smoke.*)

Signa Three   *(noun)*
A machine developed by Telecredit, Inc., that uses light technology to detect forgeries in almost anything. The Signa Three is being tested for its ability to detect fake stock certificates and securities by banking institutions.

signature dynamics   *(noun)*
A biometric technology that electronically measures the whole act of signing, not just the signature, which is easily forged. Signature dynamics considers the pressure of the pen, the speed of the hand, and any small variations in movement; an individual's signature dynamic is almost impossible to duplicate and may be incorporated into a "smart" credit card for positive identification.

silent reefer   *(noun)*
A tractor-trailer designed to ship perishable cargoes without a refrigeration unit. The silent reefer, which has double metal walls with a vacuum between them, is both more efficient and cheaper to operate than a traditional reefer.

Silkworm   *(noun)*
A mobile, twenty foot antiship missile manufactured in China and sold in quantity by China to Iran, which used it against shipping in the so-called "tanker war" in the Persian Gulf.

SilverStone™   *(noun)*
A chemically stable resin similar to Teflon, which is applied to cooking utensils to prevent food from sticking to them.

Simplesse   *(noun)*
(See *Olestra.*)

sit-comm   *(noun)*
Situation commercial. Virtually indistinguishable from TV family sitcoms, sit-comms feature titles, miniplots, stock char-

acters, and canned laughter, all squeezed into a commercial spot.

skinhead   *(noun)*
A member of a white-supremacist youth gang whose affiliates shave their heads and wear Nazi insignia as their trademark. Skinheads have been involved in many incidents of anti-Semitic and racial violence, harassment, and vandalism in the U.S., Britain, and Germany.

skit   *(noun)*
Trendy term for something that is fake, a joke. As in "Kurt says he's re-reading Proust. What a skit." (*7 Days*)

skotey   SKOH-tee   *(noun)*
Acronym for spoiled kid of the eighties. Skoteys, according to *The Wall Street Journal*, are the "baby-boom kids of the baby boom." The paper reported that this "class of [the year] 2000," numbers ten million five-to-seven-year-old children and comprises 4.2 percent of the U.S. population.

skunk works   *(noun)*
Backroom operations that companies create to foster innovation. A recent management fad, these shadow teams of researchers and managers seek to "create new products or rethink strategies outside the usual corporate setting." (*The New York Times*)

slam dance   *(noun)*
A type of punk-rock dance involving the energetic crashing of dancers into one another.

slammer   *(noun)*
In a telephone sales "boiler room" operation, the slammer is the expert high-pressure salesman who makes the pitch. Once a telephone canvasser has located a potential client, the slammer (also called the "yakker") takes over to close the deal.

slave tail   *(noun)*
The little tail of long strands of hair left hanging at the nape of the neck of boys and young men with otherwise short hair, or crew cuts.

sleaze factor   *(noun)*
Term used by critics of the Reagan administration to describe the widespread charges of ethical impropriety involving many high-ranking officials.

sleeper effect   *(noun)*
A phenomenon uncovered by psychologists studying methods of persuasion. Testers found that when subjects were given a message and then immediately told that the message was false, the subjects later remembered only the message, not its disclaimer, thus demonstrating the "sleeper," or delayed, effect.

Slick 32   *(noun)*
SLQ-32 electronic-warfare system employed by the U.S. Navy. The Slick 32 is designed to identify strange aircraft by their radar emissions.

slime suit   *(noun)*
An experimental new bathing suit of black Lycra, saturated with a water soluble gel-like substance, to make the fabric slippery when wet. Tests indicated that the suit could knock about two seconds off a swimmer's time in a 100-yard event. The gel will last for about five races.

slippery water   *(noun)*
Water with the addition of tiny amounts of a polymer, a material characterized by its long molecular structure. Researchers have discovered that the polymer significantly reduces the friction of water flowing through a pipe and naval architects are investigating the phenomenon as a technique to reduce drag on ships.

slotting allowance   *(noun)*
A fee charged by a supermarket chain to a manufacturer for the privilege of having display and shelf space for new products.

The supermarkets claim that the fees are necessary to cover their expense in handling new merchandise, but some marketers fear that the payments will make it impossible for small companies to compete.

smart card   *(noun)*
A plastic card developed in France that looks like an ordinary credit card but that contains a microprocessor capable of holding a file of bank balances, insurance, financial, and medical records, or security codes for access to computer data bases.

smart fluids   *(noun)*
Electrically activated fluids developed at the University of Michigan that can turn from liquid to solid and back again almost instantaneously. Smart fluids are expected to have significant application in robotics and automotive design.

smokeless cigarette   *(noun)*
A cigarette developed by RJR Nabisco that burns pure charcoal instead of tobacco. The smoke consists largely of carbon monoxide and water vapor, which passes through a "flavor capsule" containing tobacco extract and aromatics, and a filter made from tobacco. The resulting smoke contains nicotine but no tar, which reduces the risk of cancer and emphysema. The risks of inhaling carbon monoxide regularly, however, are not negligible.

sneeze guard   *(noun)*
A transparent glass or Plexiglas hood designed to protect uncovered salad bars in restaurants and grocery stores from direct exposure to customers' breath, while allowing access to the food for self-service.

SNOWMAX™   *(noun)*
Freeze-dried powdered bacteria used in making artificial snow at ski areas.

snuff zone   *(noun)*
No-smoking area. (*Variety*)

social investing *(noun)*
The practice of investing only in funds or companies that the investor considers morally and ethically sound, companies that have good labor practices and environmental policies, for example, or those that eschew dealing with countries whose policies are distasteful to the investor, such as South Africa.

softgel *(noun)*
A soft gelatin capsule for medication. Unlike hard, two-piece medical capsules, softgels are filled and formed into a seamless, tamper-proof pill in one operation.

soft targets *(noun)*
Literally, people—in the terminology of weapons designers.

somoclonal variation *(noun)*
A biotechnology technique of growing plant cells in special nutrients to produce a variety of characteristics—a speeding-up of natural selection. The differentiated cells are grown into whole plants so the desirability of their new properties can be studied.

songbird *(noun)*
Slang for informer. "The government says the songbird was Boyd L. Jefferies, former head of the Los Angeles brokerage firm Jefferies & Co." (*Newsweek*)

sound bite *(noun)*
A short piece of videotape excerpted as significant or representative of an event and shown repeatedly on newscasts. "The network sound bites indeed featured Reagan's lapses. . . ." (*Newsweek*)

spacebridge *(noun)*
A television program featuring a series of live, uncensored conversations between U.S. congressmen and top officials of the Soviet government. The initial programs were produced in 1987 by ABC-TV and shown live and unedited in both countries.

space junk   *(noun)*
The debris left in orbit around the earth from human efforts to get into space. Spent rockets, dead satellites, and miscellaneous objects jettisoned or lost from various spacecraft present a hazard to astronauts.

spaghetti   *(noun)*
A computer software program that has been coded with a conflicting and confusing set of commands.

spaghetti suit   *(noun)*
Water-cooled long underwear worn by astronauts. Cooling water is circulated through hundreds of feet of mini-tubing woven into the fabric.

Spelling Ace™   *(noun)*
A hand-held computer from the Franklin Computer Company that contains an 80,000-word dictionary and a pattern-matching technology that enables it to function as a spelling checker. When a word with uncertain spelling is typed into its tiny keyboard, the Spelling Ace responds with a list of correctly spelled words that seem close. If blanks are left for unknown letters, the computer will supply all the words that fit the pattern—making the machine an excellent crossword puzzle solver.

Spetsnaz   SPETS-nahz   *(noun)*
An elite Soviet special-commando force trained in surveillance, sabotage, and assassination by the KGB to attack enemy military sites at the onset of any major East-West conflict.

spin control   *(noun)*
The effort of a press agent or public relations expert to impart a favorable slant, or *spin*, to a news story relating to a client. Such a practitioner is a *spin doctor*, or *spinmaster*.

SPOCK   *(noun)*
The Special Purpose Operational Computing Kernel, an interceptor- pilot training device under development at Georgia Tech.

sports bar *(noun)*
A bar catering specifically to sports fans. Seating from 500 to 900 customers, usually with high ceilings and bleacher-style seating, the venues offer satellite-fed giant TV screens with surround sound, along with numerous monitors to allow fans to keep track of other games around the country.

spy dust *(noun)*
A chemical substance allegedly used by the KGB as a tracking powder. Sprinkled on clothing, doorknobs, or other equipment of the target, the invisible dust leaves a trail visible by ultraviolet light. In spite of news stories and diplomatic furor, tracking powders are far less efficient than modern elecronic techniques and their health hazards are negligible.

squawk *(verb)*
To transmit automatic radio or radar identification signals from an aircraft.

squeal rule *(noun)*
The controversial Department of Health, Education, and Welfare ruling that doctors must report to parents any request by a minor for contraception.

SS-24 *(noun)*
A mobile missile system deployed by the U.S.S.R. that is mounted on special railroad trains. The SS-24 has a variable range and carries ten warheads capable of being independently targeted.

starer *(noun)*
The outside man for a crack house. The starer acts as a screener of potential customers, refusing admission to anybody he thinks might be an undercover policeman.

'steenth *(noun)*
A contraction of sixteenth, frequently used in stock and commodity price quotes on the Financial News Network; "...down three 'steenths."

Stetro™   *(noun)*
Trademarked name for a plastic knob with finger indentations that slides onto a pencil shaft. The device is said to make it easier and more comfortable for children to hold a pencil properly and naturally.

stevioside   STEE-vee-oh-side   *(noun)*
A naturally occurring low-calorie sweetener from the plant *Stevia*; much sweeter than sugar but without the aftertaste of saccharin.

stick it   *(verb)*
To land on one's feet—literally or figuratively—solidly and effortlessly. The phrase comes from the world of gymnastics, where it means to return to the mat after a flip as though there were a spike extending from the bottom of each foot; thus, to land without wavering. "How was your first day on the job?" "Great, I stuck it."

stick test   *(noun)*
A do-it-yourself home-pregnancy test being marketed by several pharmaceutical companies.

strapped   *(adjective)*
Street-gang slang for being armed. "And everybody was always strapped: Magnum .45s, standard 9mms. Some guys would specialize in machine guns" (from an interview with a gang member in *U.S. News and World Report*).

street sweep   *(noun)*
A corporate takeover stragegy involving the purchase of enormous blocks of a target company's stock—"sweeping the Street"—all at once rather than making gradual acquisitions. The practice may soon be prohibited by the Securities and Exchange Commission, which suspects, along with some experts and some members of Congress, that small shareholders are hurt by it.

stride angle *(noun)*
"The maximum opening between the front and back thigh [as
a runner strides forward]," says Bob Prichard, a scientist studying the biomechanics of running. "Good sprinters will be up
around 110 or 115 degrees, and top marathoners are usually
around 90 degrees."

stupid *(adjective)*
Rap word for terrific, wonderful.

stylin' *(adjective)*
Surfer lingo for fantastic, great. (See *radical.*)

sug *(verb)*
Acronym for sell under the guise of market research, used most
frequently in Britain. "It would be surprising if at some time or
other you had not been sugged," said the *Financial Times*, which
defined sugging as "the action of unscrupulous salesmen . . .
posing as market research interviewers."

supercollider *(noun)*
A giant atom-smasher planned for construction in the United
States. The $4.4 billion superconducting supercollider will be
the most expensive scientific research tool ever built; several
states are vying for the project, both for its prestige and for the
thousands of jobs involved. The machine will be housed in a
tunnel fifty-two miles in circumference and covering twelve
thousand acres, which would require the displacing of many
families, especially in the crowded east.

superdelegate *(noun)*
A delegate to a national political convention who is not chosen
in a primary or caucus but is seated automatically as an elected
official or party leader. There were 672 superdelegates at the
1988 Democratic National Convention at Atlanta, Ga.

Super Tuesday *(noun)*
The second Tuesday in March in a U.S. election year, on which
presidential primaries are held in twenty states plus American
Samoa. The Super Tuesday states are Alabama, Arkansas,

Florida, Georgia, Hawaii, Idaho, Kentucky, Louisiana, Maryland, Massachusetts, Mississippi, Missouri, Nevada, North Carolina, Oklahoma, Rhode Island, Tennessee, Virginia, Washington, and Texas, the biggest prize in the contest because of its large number of convention votes.

surimi   suh-REE-mee   *(noun)*
Imitation shellfish meat made from shredded fish, mostly pollock. The product originated in Japan, where enormous quantities are consumed, and is becoming popular in the U.S. Surimi, in its various disguises, closely resembles crabmeat, shrimp, or lobster in appearance and flavor.

survival game   *(noun)*
A mock-combat game for adults in which two teams in combat fatigues and boots try to capture each other's flag, ambushing, and eliminating their "enemies" with air guns that fire paint capsules.

Swatch™   *(noun)*
A bright-colored plastic wristwatch designed to appeal to the under- twenty-five consumer.

swath   *(noun)*
Acronym for small waterline area, twin hull ship. Designed to give a stable ride in very rough water, swath ships have twin cigar-shaped hulls, which travel ten feet underwater. The engines are in the hulls, and the deck and passenger area are supported eight feet above the surface on struts, insulating them from surface turbulence and wave drag. The U.S. Navy has ordered a swath ship for antisubmarine warfare.

SWAY™   *(noun)*
A new Japanese fabric that changes color with the temperature. SWAY is nylon coated with microscopic capsules of thermosensitive dye that is red below 50°F, pink from 50° to 66°, and blue above that, with other color combinations available with different dyes. The fabric is being promoted for skiwear and bathing suits.

sweeps   *(noun)*
The months set by the Neilsen and Arbitron TV rating services—November, February, and May—to establish the rank-
ing of the television network shows, which determines the
advertising rates for local stations. The networks schedule their
top shows for the sweeps in order to look good in the ratings.

swoon stock   *(noun)*
Stock-market term for an extremely sensitive security that is
prone to "swoon" at bad news and rumors, causing its value to
drop drastically.

synthpop   *(noun)*
Pop music as interpreted on a synthesizer by such performers
as Grammy Award-winner Howard Jones, one of the stars of
the new generation of technician-musicians.

T

tablescape   *(noun)*
A scene created by the placement of decorative objects, books, photographs, etc., on a surface such as a bookcase, piano, shelf, or table; used primarily in interior decorating.

table setters   *(noun)*
In baseball, the first two hitters of the lineup, whose job it is to get on base ("set the table") for the sluggers who follow them.

tagine   ta-JEEN   *(noun)*
A North African stew now appearing on U.S. menus. Tagines, which usually contain lamb and vegetables, are named after the pot in which they are cooked.

talkback   *(noun)*
A new theatrical practice in which audience members are invited to comment on a production after the final curtain, giving the director and company fresh insights.

tapped out   *(adjective)*
Without money; drained of financial resources.

Taser   *(noun)*
The trademarked acronym for Tom Swift and his electric rifle, a stun gun used by police departments to immobilize violent suspects. The Taser, which resembles a flashlight, fires two tiny

darts carrying fifty-thousand volts into a subject's body from fifteen feet away, disabling him or her without permanent effects.

T-ball   *(noun)*
A simple version of baseball for five- to seven-year-old children in which the batter hits the ball off a waist-high tee instead of trying to hit a pitched ball.

TCAS   *(noun)*
Abbreviation for Traffic Collision Avoidance System, a trademarked electronic device that permits an airplane pilot to determine the range, bearing, and altitude of an approaching aircraft, thus decreasing the risk of high-altitude collisions.

TDF   *(noun)*
Abbreviation for testes-determining factor, the name given by scientists to the recently discovered gene on the Y chromosome normally found in male cells. The TDF gene is believed to be the trigger that, when present in the fertilized egg, will cause the fetus to develop as a male, and when absent, as a female.

technotrash   *(noun)*
Computerists' slang term for a person who is gifted technically but who has a disagreeable personality and behaves boorishly.

Teflon   *(adjective)*
The property, named for the trademarked antistick resin used on cooking utensils, that enables its possessor to shed with ease the effects of bad times and get credit for good; commonly applied to Ronald Reagan's immunity from the traditional laws of politics, as in "the Teflon factor" (*Newsweek*), or "the Teflon presidency" (*Washington Post*).

teleoperators   *(noun)*
Experimental microscopic tools that when inserted into an artery on a catheter will enable surgeons to perform surgery by remote control.

teletheater   *(noun)*
An elite off-track-betting establishment with a restaurant, a bar, and several giant television screens providing live coverage of the races. Teletheaters charge a five-dollar admission, but there is no five percent surcharge on winnings as in the standard OTB parlors.

Temaki   teh-MAH-kee   *(noun)*
A new speaker from Mitsubishi in the form of a flat sheet of piezoelectric resin that vibrates under electrical stimulation, producing sound. Temakis, named for their resemblance to the sheets of seaweed used in making temaki sushi, may be mounted behind a framed picture and hung on the wall.

temp   *(noun)*
A worker employed on a temporary basis. American corporations are using increasing numbers of temps as part of cost-cutting strategy; these workers usually receive no expensive fringe benefits and can be quickly let go when the workload decreases.

tent pole movie   *(noun)*
"A surefire hit [movie] to help support your entire season schedule," according to Frank Mancuso, studio chief of Paramount.

terrorilla   *(noun)*
A name that Israeli officials have given to the combination of *terror*ism and guer*rilla* warfare confronting Israeli forces in southern Lebanon.

that dog don't hunt   *(colloquialism)*
An expression of disbelief in the validity of a stated belief or argument, or in the viability of an idea.

three-hump camel   *(noun)*
U.S. military slang for the outcome of an attempt by all three branches to collaborate in building a single weapon.

TICK   *(noun)*
Acronym for two-income couple with kids.

tin man   *(noun)*
Nickname for the all-aluminum AX-5 experimental spacesuit.
(See *Mark 3*.)

tin parachute   *(noun)*
A plan that guarantees a company's rank-and-file employees,
depending on their tenure, severance pay in the event of a
hostile takeover of the company. The money would have to be
honored by the new management, making a takeover more
expensive. Tin parachute is a spinoff of "golden parachute"—
the lucrative guarantee often given to top executives.

tiramisu   terra-MEE-soo   *(noun)*
An Italian dessert that varies with the whim of the creator but
that is basically sponge cake soaked with espresso, filled with
a mixture of Italian double-cream cheese blended with eggs and
sugar, and topped with slivered bittersweet chocolate or cocoa.

Tofutti™   tuh-FOO-tee   *(noun)*
The trademarked name for tofu "ice cream." Invented by
Brooklyn entrepreneur David Mintz, it is a dairy-free dessert
for consumers who keep kosher and cannot eat meat and dairy
food at the same meal, and a viable dessert alternative for
people on low cholesterol or low-lactose diets.

tombstone   *(noun)*
A Wall Street ad for, among other purposes, announcing new
stock issues. The tombstone is so named because it gives only
bare-bones facts, as on a monument, leaving details for the
stock's prospectus or other legally required documents.

topline   *(verb)*
To star in, get top billing. "Dennis Cole toplines in Peter Uval's
[movie] *Dead End City*." (*Variety*)

topper   *(noun)*
Film industry term for chief executive. "National Film Development Corporation topper Malati Tambay-Vaidya was in high
spirits over the three Indian films scattered throughout the
Cannes program." (*Variety*)

toxic waste   *(noun)*
The hazardous by-products of chemical and manufacturing industries. Because toxic wastes pose a threat to health and the environment, methods for their disposal are a volatile political subject in the United States.

toyetic   *(adjective)*
Having a potential for being translated into a popular toy, as, for example, the movie character Rambo or the characters and gadgets from the *Star Wars* films.

TR   *(noun)*
Abbreviation for treasury receipt, a type of *zero* coupon bond.

tradecraft   *(noun)*
Term used in the intelligence community for the body of knowledge and skills necessary for an agent to operate successfully undercover.

train surfing   *(noun)*
The dangerous practice among Rio's poor of riding hanging onto the outside of trains.

transformer   *(noun)*
A popular toy that "transforms" into different shapes with totally different characteristics. A robot, for example, may be changed into a jet fighter by manipulating ingeniously hinged and swiveled plastic parts.

transition game   *(noun)*
The point in a basketball game at which the two sides switch, respectively, from offense to defense; a key buzzword in eighties basketball. Teams adept at the transition game are usually well supplied with *greyhounds* and are generally known as *run-and-gun-teams*; teams less able at the transition game are likely to be stocked with "plodders"—big, slow players—and prefer to play a "halfcourt" game (to be slow in setting up their offense).

transition rule *(noun)*
A Capitol Hill euphemism for a special tax break inserted in a bill with the object of winning support from a certain legislator by giving tax exemptions to a favored project in his or her home district.

trash-to-energy system *(noun)*
An electric power plant fueled with garbage or trash, burned at extremely high temperatures. The intense heat is said to destroy odors and pollutants and, not incidentally, to destroy the trash. In increasing use in such cities as Boston, whose trash-to-energy system consumes twelve hundred tons of refuse per day.

tree-hugger *(noun)*
Epithet for a radical environmentalist.

triathatard try-ATH-uh-tard *(noun)*
A one-piece space-age-fabric exercise suit that hugs the body from neck to ankle. Similar to leotards, triathatards, which take their name from the triathlon, are also known as "skinsuits."

triple witching hour *(noun)*
The Friday every three months when stock options, stock index options, and futures on index options all come due, creating a very volatile market as traders scramble to close out their positions.

Trivial Pursuit™ *(noun)*
A popular board game base on questions and answers about miscellaneous facts from historical and contemporary culture.

trojan horse *(noun)*
A high-tech computer-spying technique in which an apparently legitimate program is inserted into a computer. The bogus program feigns normal activity but actually can be rigged for all sorts of illicit functions, from outright sabotage to stealing information.

tropicalism   *(noun)*
The synthesis of popular Brazilian music with elements from jazz, rock, and Caribbean music.

Trump Card   *(noun)*
A business card marketed by Positive Concepts Ltd., of Atlanta, Georgia, that features a personal, color photograph of its holder—to give viewers a memorable, individualized impression.

truppie   *(noun)*
An upscale trucker who takes his or her family life on the road in living quarters behind the truck cab. Husband-and-wife teams can spell each other at the wheel, doubling both time on the road and distance covered—important with perishable cargoes. Truppie cabins are up to ten feet long and sometimes better equipped than most motor homes. Although a really elaborate compartment can cost as much as $40,000, savings on highway food and lodging—not to mention the beneficial effect on truppies' marriages—can make it worthwhile.

tube steak   *(noun)*
Slang for hot dog.

Tubby   *(noun)*
A mutual fund named after I. W. "Tubby" Burnham II, of Drexel Burnham Lambert. Other brokerage houses are developing their own version of the Tubby.

tweener   *(noun)*
A hit in baseball that lands between two outfielders, too far away from either player to be fielded. ABC newsman Bill O'Reilly used the word to characterize people between social classes. "Tweeners are people who have come from working-class upbringings, and have become successful professionals through hard work and education but have not abandoned their roots."

12th man   *(noun)*
The name given the kick-coverage team by coach Jackie Sherrill of the Texas A&M football team. Although not yet in widespread use, it may catch on.

Type T   *(adjective)*
A psychological classification for a personality type that seeks stimulation and risks—T for thrill-seeking. According to psychologists, Type Ts are capable of being either unusually creative, finding their excitement in mental exercise, or exceptionally destructive, getting their kicks from such socially unacceptable activities as crime and violent behavior.

U

ultra *(noun)*
Advertising-trade jargon, short for ultraconsumer and referring to purchasers who insist on the best of everything, regardless of their income—people with "champagne appetites,"
always optimistically pursuing an affluent style of living.

Ultraphone™ *(noun)*
A digital radiotelephone that transmits messages in digital
code, by radio, to a standard telephone company. The device
makes it possible for people in remote areas to have phone
service.

underwater *(adjective)*
The condition in which the exercise price of a stock option is
higher than the market price because of a falling market. Stock
options granted to executives as fringe benefits become worth-
less in the underwater condition since it would cost more to
exercise the option than the stock is worth.

unimog YOON-uh-mog *(noun)*
A street-cleaning device coming into use in U.S. cities. The
machine, sometimes called a "super truck," is said to be capable
of vacuuming between parked cars, plowing or inhaling snow,
spreading salt, and compacting trash. "It looks," reported *The
New York Times*, "like the offspring of a garbage truck mated

with a vacuum cleaner, and it emits an unearthly, ear-shattering noise."

unspool   *(verb)*
To screen a film, in show-biz slang.

urgicenter   URJ-uh-sent-er   *(noun)*
An emergency outpatient medical clinic providing treatment for health problems that do not require hospitalization.

user interface   *(noun)*
The technology of symbols and commands with which an operator interacts with a computer.

utilization management   *(noun)*
Techniques used by efficiency experts for analyzing and improving productivity.

V

vacherin   VASH-ran   *(noun)*
Prized by connoisseurs, vacherin is a soft-ripened, richly flavored cow's-milk cheese from the Swiss Alps, made only in the fall and available only in the winter.

vanilla   *(adjective)*
Plain and unadorned, or flat or bland, describing anything from a basic car to a lackluster performance.

Vegemite™   VEJ-i-mite   *(noun)*
An extremely popular Australian food product made from yeast. Gaining acceptance in some parts of the United States, the thick, black paste has a salty flavor and is used both as a spread and a flavor enhancer.

VH1   *(noun)*
Abbreviation for Video Hits One, a cable-TV channel carrying music videos. VH1 is aimed at the over-thirty audience as an alternative to the more energetic and raucous MTV rock and roll music videos designed for the under-thirty viewer.

VideOcart   *(noun)*
A high-tech advertising device that attaches to a supermarket shopping cart. The VideOcart is a screen keyed to sensors on store shelves, which displays ads for the products it passes. The screens can also transmit other customer-service information, as desired by the store management.

video club   *(noun)*
A lounge or café where the entertainment consists of videos shown on numerous television screens.

videodical   vid-ee-ODD-uh-kal   *(noun)*
A regularly issued special-interest videocassette. Available by subscription and through stores and newsstands, videodicals are aimed at such groups as auto-racing enthusiasts, young adults and outdoor- sports fans.

video yearbook   *(noun)*
A videocassette version of the school yearbook. Video yearbooks are made from edited footage taped throughout the year and supplied with a sound track and graphics.

virus   *(noun)*
A computer program hidden on a floppy disk that contaminates the computer's master program. Viruses remain hidden and may invade every new disk used in the computer. While some are merely jokes and surface as a comic message or graphic, others are programmed to destroy or change stored data. (See *trojan horse*.)

visualization   *(noun)*
A psychological training technique widely used by competitive athletes to improve their skills. Visualization consists of imagining an ideal performance over and over and forming a mental image of oneself duplicating it.

voice lineup   *(noun)*
A method that enables a witness to identify a criminal suspect by hearing a tape of the subject's voice.

vulture fund   *(noun)*
An investment mutual fund that acquires underutilized or empty buildings and other troubled real estate properties at bargain prices with a view to increasing their value through better management.

W

wack   *(adjective)*
Bad, dreadful. Hip-hop pejorative seen on graffiti wall: "Crack is wack!"

wallyball   *(noun)*
A sport played with a soft ball on a walled court. Wallyball is similar to volleyball, but the softer ball can't go out of play because the walls bounce every shot back onto the court, making for a faster and more strenuous game.

wallyo   WAHL-yo   *(noun)*
An affectionate, Italian-American term for a young man.

wannabee   *(noun)*
A running together of "want to be." A wannabee is an ardent fan of a celebrity who slavishly imitates his or her idol in dress and behavior. Examples are the clones of Madonna—"Madonna wannabees"—or the surfer wannabees who dress the part but don't surf. There are similar nonparticipating fans of tennis and skiing.

warmblood   *(noun)*
A European breed of horse currently popular in the United States for crossbreeding with thoroughbreds to produce jumpers. While not eligible for racing, these crossbreeds star in show jumping.

warmedy *(noun)*
A compound of *warm* and com*edy*, used in the television in-dustry to characterize situation comedies about cozy family relationships. "Warm family comedies (or *warmedies*, as the industry now calls them) that cast a cozy glow over our memories of television's youth" (*Newsweek*).

Wasp *(noun)*
A robotlike deep-water hard diving suit. Its bright yellow color and segmented body inspired its name.

water trade *(noun)*
A Japanese term for that nation's burgeoning cafe-society busi-ness, a world of retreats where normally straitlaced customers relax and throw off the restraints of protocol under the in-fluence of liquor.

wax *(noun)*
To defeat. "The people have not seen us waxed like this in three years," said Knicks spokesman Hubie Brown after a particular-ly humiliating loss. In 1984 political columnists Rowland Evans and Robert Novak wrote about a Reagan strategist who was "ecstatic over the waxing of Walter Mondale."

wealth effect *(noun)*
The bolstering effect on the economy created by a rising stock market, which tends to encourage investors to spend some of their profits on consumer goods.

wedge buster *(noun)*
In football, a player whose job it is to break up the opposing team's array of blockers (wedge) on kickoffs, usually by hurling himself at full speed into as many opponents as possible. This player is sometimes called a "kamikaze."

wet dog *(noun)*
An officially listed term used by wine professionals to charac-terize a particular chemical aroma of some wines.

wetware   *(noun)*
Computerists' slang for the brain.

whirler   *(noun)*
A member of the super-fashionable high-society set of wealthy people conspicuous in the social "whirl."

white bread   *(adjective)*
Bland and unexciting, having the qualities of supermarket white bread. (See also *vanilla*.)

whole nine yards   *(noun)*
Everything connected with a given object or process. "The town's newest playpen is The Drinkery, a palace of preposterous trendiness that features expensive drinks, stained glass, exposed brick, hanging plants—the whole nine yards" (Saybrook *Gazette*). The phrase originated as praise for a tailor; when a patron bought the nine yards of fabric required for a suit, and the tailor, not scrimping, used all of it, he was commended for giving the "whole nine yards."

winter-beater   *(noun)*
An old, beat-up car used during the winter months to spare its owner's good car the trauma of driving on salted roads.

win-win   *(adjective)*
In Washington jargon, win-win describes an action or situation with no risk involved, like throwing one's support behind the war on drugs. A negotiating strategy where both sides gain.

WOOFS   *(noun)*
Acronym for well-off older folks, another coinage from the advertising industry, which is searching for ways to appeal to the expanding older population.

word, or word up   *(interjection)*
An informal expression of praise used like "bravo": "Word up! You did a terrific job on that book."

worm   *(noun)*
A *trojan horse* computer program designed to sabotage a computer's data storage by gradually eating away existing files as they are used.

wound laboratory   *(noun)*
The firing range of the Defense Department on the campus of the national military medical school in Bethesda, Maryland, where doctors were trained in battlefield medicine, and dogs, pigs, goats, and other animals were shot with high-powered weapons so their wounds could be studied by surgeons and scientists. Revelation of the wound lab's existence created a public outcry, and the program there was discontinued. Animal rights activists report that the "lab" has since been moved elsewhere, though dogs are no longer among those animals shot.

wrongful birth   *(noun)*
The subject of a medical-malpractice suit in which a plaintiff claims that a doctor has negligently permitted the birth of a severely handicapped child by not testing for birth defects and giving the option of abortion. All such cases to date have been disallowed, and Minnesota and Missouri have enacted laws banning wrongful-birth claims.

wunk   *(noun)*
Slang for the teenage music hits of the sixties—wasp funk— which is currently enjoying a modest revival.

wuss   *(noun)*
Slang for a weak, ineffectual person; a wimp.

Y

Yakuza *(noun)*
A Japanese crime syndicate involved in illicit activities around the world. According to California Attorney General John Van De Camp, Yakuza's international enterprises garner some $4 billion a year, money that is then invested in legitimate business and real estate.

yellow cow *(noun)*
In China, the name given to black marketeers who buy up scarce state-subsidized goods and sell them for greatly inflated prices.

Yellow Finn *(noun)*
Also Yellow Finnish, a European variety of potato that turns a golden yellow when cooked. Many feel they have a creamier texture and fuller flavor than other varities, and cholesterol-conscious consumers prefer them because they require no butter. Grown in most northern states, Yellow Finns are finding their way to produce stores and supermarkets.

yogarobics *(noun)*
A physical fitness program based on the postures and breathing exercises prescribed in the Hindu philosophy of yoga.

yokoso *(interjection)*
"Welcome," in Japanese, and likely to be used more widely in the United States to greet the record number of Japanese tourists traveling here.

Y-people *(noun)*
Yuppies. Y-people, or Y-person, is now used by many journalists, from columnists to cartoonists (such as Garry Trudeau of *Doonesbury* fame) in place of "yuppie."

yuca YUK-ka *(noun)*
Acronym for young, upwardly mobile Cuban-American.

yuffies *(noun)*
Young urban failures. According to Patty Friedmann, in her humorous book, *Too Smart To Be Rich: On Being a Yuffie*," they are brilliant underachievers who never make it financially.

Z

zap *(noun)*
A protest demonstration designed to get maximum media attention focused on the AIDS issue and on the organizations that activists believe are lax in their efforts to combat AIDS. (See *ACT UP.*)

ZapMail *(noun)*
Trade name used by the Federal Express Corporation for an electronic mail service capable of transmitting copies of correspondence across the United States in two hours or less.

zeitgeber TSITE-gay-bur *(noun)*
German for "time giver." Zeitgebers are drugs capable of resetting the body's daily rhythms. Some hypertension medicines, along with L-dopa (used in treating Parkinson's disease) and caffeine, are zeitgebers and, for proper effect, must be taken at specific times of day. According to Charles Ehret at the Argonne National Laboratory, caffeine taken in the morning advances your "clock" so that you stay up later, but it has no effect when taken between 3:30 and 5 P.M., and in the evening makes you want to retire earlier.

zero out *(verb)*
The act of not paying taxes. A wealthy person, for example, can zero out if all his or her declarable income derives from tax-exempt municipal bonds. Some corporations have been able to

use so many tax writeoffs that they have been zeroing out for years.

Zinthane *(noun)*
Trademarked name for a synthetic golf-ball covering. High-quality balls have traditionally been covered with balata, a relative of rubber obtained with great difficulty from the jungles of South America. According to *The New York Times*, golfer Greg Norman, who has won more than $1 million dollars with a Zinthane ball, calls it "the ball of the future."

Zip *(noun)*
An American-based, Sicilian-born gangster. Sicilian mafiosi— Zips—have been actively recruited by some older U.S. mafia chiefs, who feel that the old "family" codes are being eroded by the penchant for high living among young American-born mobsters.

zone *(noun)*
The transcendental state of euphoria and confidence achieved by some athletes, enabling them to perform at peak mental and physical efficiency.

zoomoozophone zoo-MOO-zuh-fone *(noun)*
A musical instrument similar to a vibraphone, the zoomoozophone is designed to play music in the microtonal 31-note scale.

zouk zuke *(noun)*
Caribbean rock dance music from the French Antilles.

INDEX

Abbreviations, Acronyms, and Portmanteau Words

The Arts, Entertainment

Afro-pop
ambisonic
Arkie
Artagraph
artspeak
artsport
B-boy
b-girl
boudoir photography
capoeira
cassingle
CD-videos
chatcom
checkerboarding
cheers
chopsocky
Christian pop
Claymation
confrotalk
cruciverbalist
Deadheads
dramedy
dwarf-throwing
ear candy
electrofunk
environmental theater
first-sale doctrine
flyover people
F/X
gorilla
graphic novel
HDV
installation
interactive toy
karaoke
kidult

kurogo
life cast
living movie
manga
maximinimalism
metalhead
minimal miking
moonwalk
movideo
multimiking
Neo-Geo
new-age music
panto
pathography
people meter
PIP
praisery
preem
promenade theater
pubcaster
Radio Marti
rai
ranchera
ribbon speaker
sandwich music
shakuhachi
shock jock
Showscan
sit-comm
slam dance
sound bite
spacebridge
sports bar
survival game
sweeps
synthpop

Business and Finance

affinity card
A-list
American Eagle
arb
Automation Alley
barter advertising
beltway bandit
Black Monday
Bowash
breakup value
cafeteria plan
cascade
churn and burn
competitor analysis
critical path
dividend capture
dockominium
DRIP
factory farming
feemail
first-sale doctrine
fixed mix
flanker
flipper
focus group
Fortune 500
401(k) plan
FSI
golden handcuff
greenshoe
G-7
hell camp
insider trading
IRMA
January effect
J-curve

JOA
just-in-time
killer technology
LBO
Libertad
lollipop
maquiladora
mechatronics
megadink
ministorage
MMDA
mommy track
mooch
naked short-selling
new-collar
operateur
orangemail
Pac-Man defense
Panda
peewee tech
pink collar
pink sheets
podmall
portfolio insurance
power breakfast
price-sales ratio
program trading
prosumer
puddle
quant
rain insurance
rocket scientist
scorched earth
securitization
shark repellent
short-swing rule

Computers

Agenda
agrimation
Arkie
Automation Alley
baseband
Big Floyd
biochip
CASE
CD-I
CD-ROM
computer hedgehog
computer monitoring
cracker
DRAMS
electronic cadavers
electronic cottage
Etak Navigator
fifth-generation computer
Herzog keyboard
hypertext
mechatronics

Micropacer
MIDI
Minitel
MMIC
MTSO
Oedipus
optical processor
parallel processing
peewee tech
phreaking
program trading
rocket scientist
shareware
smart card
spaghetti
Spelling Ace
SPOCK
trojan horse
virus
worm

Criminal and Legal

Argentine method
battered wife syndrome
bazuko
Big Floyd
black tar
blazing seat
bomb blanket
Bubba Law
bubble
CAMP
C-4
checkbook witness
churn and burn
coke bugs
crackhead
cryptomnesia
crystal meth
date-rape
death-qualify
deep pocket
devastator
DNA fingerprints
drive-by
DVP
first-sale doctrine
FIST
flutter
fourth degree
full field
Glock 17
Guardian Angels
hippo
hubba
insider trading

Jade Squad
marital rape
mommy track
mooch
narcokleptocracy
orangemail
Pamyat
phreaking
posse
progun
riot shield
rocket docket
sanctuary movement
script writer
shank
short-swing rule
Signa Three
signature dynamics
skinhead
sleaze factor
songbird
spy dust
squeal rule
starer
strapped
street sweep
Taser
trojan horse
voice lineup
worm
wrongful birth
Yakuza
yellow cow
Zip

Environment

afterburst
agrigenetics
agrimation
animal rights movement
bioremediation
bubble concept
butterfly effect
clamshell
coyote
ducting
Ecolyte
ecotage
facadism
hummocks
hush kit
linear park

omnicide
petracide
PSI
radon daughters
Rails-to-Trails Conservancy
red-bag waste
rehaber
rockplowing
secondhand smoke
sick building
sidestream smoke
SNOWMAX
toxic waste
trash-to-energy system
tree-hugger
unimog

Food and Drink

agrigenetics
agrimation
akachochin
appliance garage
aristology
asham
atemoya
bammie
banger
beer ball
Belgian Blue
bellini
biobone
blackened fish
blaff
blue-corn chips
blush wine
boruga
brew pub
Bubba Law
Cajun popcorn
cavaillon
dry beer
dry-season gardening
factory farming
fluffy cellulose
focaccia
frogmore stew
galaktobouriko
green serpent

horchata
impitoyable
LA
lumen
monoammonium glutamate
nopalitos
nori
Nu-Trish a-B
Olestra
penne
playfood
pour
power breakfast
runza
sakau
samogon
SilverStone
Simplesse
sneeze guard
stevioside
surimi
tagine
tiramisu
Tofutti
tube steak
vacherin
Vegemite
water trade
wet dog
Yellow Finn

Health and Medicine

International Affairs

Language

allophone
ankle
artspeak
B and T crowd
BEV
bogart
bum-rush
cascade
cheers
chopsocky
confrotalk
cruciverbalist
def
dis
dope
Ebonics
English creep
fresh
fuzzword
fuzzy sets
grok
homes
hood
house
kick back
la langue du Coca-Cola

lexigram
mamou
mommy track
motherese
Oedipus
. . . or what?
packwood
peredishka
perestroika
poco
precip
Seaspeak
skit
Spelling Ace
spin control
stupid
Teflon
vanilla
wack
wax
white bread
whole nine yards
wuss
yokoso
Y-people
yuca

Life-Style

acid wash
advid
affinity card
Agenda
A-list
aristology
aromatherapy
artspeak
artsport
banger
bazuko
belt bag
black tar
boomerang
botanica
boudoir photography
Bubba Law
camel
capsule hotel
Christian pop
cocooning
coke bugs
couch people
Couch Potato
crackhead
cross-training
date-rape
D.B.
DENK
designated driver
DEWK
dink
dockominium
dogolatry
dwarf-throwing
ear candy

Ebonics
ecotage
eldercare
electronic cottage
Eurostyle
femmenism
15-minute celebrity
Filofax
fiver
Flashing
flex
fluffing out
flyover people
freezenik
frontloading
gateway drug
gîte
granola
greenfly
grippers
group-bridging
guanxi
Harold
hipo
homeboy
hothousing
Joe Six-pack
kiddie condo
laundermat-bar
lemon tart
linear park
loop
male bonding
manga
matures
minidorm

Management and Organization

baseband
birdcage
cafeteria plan
CAMP
computer monitoring
critical path
DRIP
factory farming
flex
flexible freeze
fluffing out
flutter
Fortune 500
401(k) plan
golden handcuff
go-go
goo-goo
greenshoe

hell camp
just-in-time
loop
maquiladora
micromanagement
mommy track
operateur
perestroika
scorched earth
screwdriver plant
shark repellent
shurocracy
skunk world
slotting allowance
TCAS
topper
utilization management
Yakuza

The Media

advid
animal
Arabsat
beat sweetener
chatcom
checkbook journalism
checkerboarding
confrotalk
dayparting
dramedy
flyover people
Fortune 500
FSI
F/X
grip-and-grin
HDV
magalog
manga

MOS bite
people meter
PIP
pool reporter
pour
praisery
pubcaster
Radio Marti
shock jock
sit-comm
sound bite
spacebridge
spin control
sweeps
VH1
VideOcart
videodical
warmedy

The Military

afterburst
Argentine method
arms supermarket
backpack nuke
beltway bandit
bodywash
boomer
dense pack
devastator
East Wind
Energia
Euromissile
go-go
heavy bead
Hexapod
hippo
Hummer

Killer Egg
krytron
living fence
micromanagement
mini-RVP
Old Crows
painted
petracide
SEALS
soft targets
Silkworm
Slick 32
SPOCK
SS-24
terrorilla
three-hump camel
wound laboratory

Movements and Causes

ACT UP
animal rights movement
Big Floyd
designated drivers
ecotage
fiver
freezenik
Intact Baby Movement
intifada
Marantha
necklacing
Neo-Geo
new age

Notch Baby
Opus Dei
Pamyat
perestroika
progun
Rails-to-Trails Conservancy
Rainbow
rehaber
sanctuary movement
Santeria
skinhead
zap

Politics

A-list
allophone
animal
black spot
bracketing
D.B.
evil empire
facadism
flutter
freezenik
full-court press
fuzzword
golpe
goo-goo
grip-and-grin
guanxi
Gucci gauntlet

heavy bead
new-collar
nomenklatura
Notch Baby
oilgas'n'timber
owl
packwood
perestroika
poco
pothold politician
Reaganaut
shurocracy
sleaze factor
superdelegate
Super Tuesday
Teflon
transition rule

Products and Services

acid wash
ADRMP
advid
aeroshell
affinity card
Agenda
appliance garage
aromatherapy
Artagraph
Auto Shade
beer ball
bellini
belt bag
blue-corn chips
blush wine
Boinks
boudoir photography
bomb blanket
branded diamond
camo
capsule hotel
cassingle
CD-videos
clamshell
Congregate care
Copper T
Couch Potato
Dazer
doc-watcher
dry beer
Dungeons and Dragons
Ecolyte
econobox
ecstasy
energy return shoes
Enhanced 911

ergometer
Etak Navigator
Filofax
Flashing
front-end bra
FSI
gelcap
getaway special
gimme cap
Glock 17
Glycel
graphic novel
grippers
group-bridging
hair extension
HDV
Herzog keyboard
interactive toy
Joltmeter
karaoke
krytron
laundermat-bar
lumen
Libertad
LifeCard
manga
Micropacer
MicroTrak
ministorage
Minitel
MTSO
Olestra
OliverShield
Panda
photocard
pink sheets

Sports

Space, Science, and Nature

aeroshell
afterburst
aging gene
agrigenetics
agrimation
ambisonic
animal rights movement
anti-sense medicine
artificial gill
Bambi syndrome
Belgian Blue
biobone
bioremediation
bloodless surgery
blood scavenger
bubble concept
butterfly effect
caramel
CD4
C-4
chaos
chronopharmacology
cryobirth
Dazer
DNA fingerprints
dracontology
dry-season gardening
ducting
dustman
Ecolyte
Energia
facedness
factory farming
fifth force
Fjord
fresh-cell therapy

gene therapy
getaway special
glowboy
GM-CSF
gnat-robot
hypercharge
killer technology
krytron
LD-50
lexigram
lightsat
Mark 3
meltdown
micromachine
omnicide
ozone hole
Peter Pan syndrome
P4
pregaphone
QFIA
rehaber
resource recovery
rockplowing
rollover
rubber mirror
Sgr A*
slippery water
smart fluids
somoclonal variation
space junk
spaghetti suit
squawking
supercollider
TCAS
TDF
teleoperators

Do you have any appropriate new words, additions or suggestions for our next edition of the *Dictionary of New Words*? If so, send them to:

Sid Lerner
175 East 74th St.
New York, NY 10021

Remember, no compensation or credit can be given, and only appropriate suggestions will be included.

About the Authors

HAROLD LeMAY is a linguist, editor, painter, and sculptor. He has worked in the construction industry, the plastics business, and the book publishing trade. Mr. LeMay now installs exhibits at the Lyme Academy of Fine Art in Old Lyme, Connecticut.

SID LERNER is a book packager and new products developer with a background in advertising and a nose for trends. His first book was *Monday Morning Quarterback* and he's currently producing *From the Desk of:*, a celebrity photo book for fall '89.

MARIAN TAYLOR, currently an editor at Chelsea House Publishers, has also been an editor at the New York Times syndicate, the Los Angeles Times syndicate, and *Life* magazine.